CAMPAIGNS
LESSONS FROM THE FIELD

Edited by Wade Rathke

Copyright ©2018 by Wade Rathke
All rights reserved. No part of this publication may be reproduced, distributed, or transmitted in any form or by any means, including photocopying, recording, or other electronic or mechanical methods, without the prior written permission of the publisher, except in the case of brief quotations embodied in critical reviews and certain other non-commercial uses permitted by copyright law.

For permission requests, write to the publisher below:
Social Policy Press
2221 St. Claude Avenue, New Orleans, LA 70117 (physical)
PO Box 3924, New Orleans, LA 70177 (mailing)
Tel: (504) 302-1238
www.socialpolicypress.org

Ordering information
Quantity sales
Special discounts are available on quantity purchases by corporations, associations, and others. For details, contact the Publisher at the Social Policy address above.

Individual sales
Social Policy Press publications are available through bookstores. They can also be ordered directly from Social Policy Press at the above numbers and through socialpolicypress.org.

Orders for college textbook/course adoption use
Contact Social Policy Press (504) 302-1238

Orders for U.S. and other trade bookstores and wholesalers
Please contact Social Policy Press or visit our website.

Social Policy Press is a registered trademark of
Labor Neighbor Research and Training Center, Inc.

Printed in the United States of America.

Rathke, Wade
Campaigns: Lessons from the Field
ISBN 978-0-9970943-3-6
1. Community, labor, and political organizing
2. Actions, strategy, and tactics
3. Building mass organizations

First edition
Layout and design: Hatty Lee Lin, San Francisco, California
Copyediting: Mary Rowles, Salt Spring, British Columbia, and Joe Szakos, Charlottesville, Virginia

TABLE OF CONTENTS

INTRODUCTION 6

UNDERSTANDING AND WAGING CAMPAIGNS 14
Wade Rathke

JOBS

BAN THE BOX IN SOUTHSIDE VIRGINIA 23
Nik Belanger

EQUITY FOR HOME-BASED CAREGIVERS IN HAWAII 26
Drew Astolfi

WINNING WAGE INCREASES USING REFERENDA IN ORGANIZING 37
Lew Finfer

SUMMER JOBS FOR YOUTH: The Mission Coalition
Organization Campaign 43
Mike Miller

INCOME

POVERTY POTLUCK: Battling Social Assistance Clawbacks in Canada 48
Claire Gallagher

MINIMUM STANDARDS CAMPAIGNS 51
Wade Rathke and Bill Pastreich

FURNITURE FOR FAMILIES 55
Steven Kest and Wade Rathke

IT'S EXPENSIVE TO BE POOR: Fighting Predatory Lending 57
Judy Duncan

HEALTH

USING COMMUNITY ORGANIZING STRATEGIES
TO FIGHT HOSPITAL DEBT IN WASHINGTON 62
LeeAnn Hall

THE AMBULANCE PLEDGE CARD SYSTEM 68
Zach Polett

HOUSING
LANDLORD LICENSING IN CANADA 72
John Anderson and Marva Burnett

FIGHTING FOR RENT CONTROL IN SANTA ROSA 78
Davin Cardenas

ORGANIZING FOR WATER RIGHTS IN THE PARIS SUBURBS 81
Adrien Roux

PROPOSITION H: Building Tenant Power in San Francisco 83
Randy Shaw

ACORN HOME SAVERS CAMPAIGN: Old Wine in New Bottles? 87
Dine' Butler and Wade Rathke

TENANTS CASH-IN BY BREAKING THE BLACK MARKET IN ROME 90
David Tozzo

RIGHTS AND SAFETY CAMPAIGNS FOR WOMEN, YOUTH, AND IMMIGRANTS
RAPE, RESISTANCE, AND ORGANIZING 95
Beth Butler with Ruth Rinehart

STUDENTS WIN LGBTQ RIGHTS AT CHARLOTTESVILLE SCHOOLS 99
Joe Szakos

IMMIGRANTS' RIGHTS STRENGTHENED IN LAWRENCE, MASSACHUSETTS 104
Emily Bloch

TAXES AND CITY SERVICES
BLOCKING THE BRISTOL COUNCIL TAX 110
Nick Ballard and Anny Cullum

LEVELING THE FIELD ON PROPERTY TAX EQUALIZATION   116
Steven Kest and Wade Rathke

DON'T BE A BLOCKHEAD   117
Robert Fisher, Fred Brooks, and Daniel Russell

SAVE THE CITY CAMPAIGN: Winning Centennial Park in Little Rock   130
Steven Kest and Wade Rathke

LAND AND RESOURCES
FIVE COUNTRIES ALLIED AGAINST LAND-GRABBING   133
Eloise Maulet

NOT ON MY FIELDS AND NOT FROM MY POCKETBOOK:
The White Bluff Power Plant Campaign   140
Wade Rathke and Steven Kest

DEVELOPMENT
EQUITABLE DEVELOPMENT COMES TO DC   144
Dominic T. Moulden and Gregory D. Squires

PULLING DEFEAT FROM VICTORY IN THE FIGHT TO BLOCK
THE Q STADIUM IN CLEVELAND   149
Randy Cunningham

ROAD BLOCK: Fighting the Freeway in Little Rock   158
Darcy Pumphrey

PARTICIPATORY PLANNING CAMPAIGN IN LAST DITCH
EFFORT TO SAVE MEMPHIS PUBLIC HOUSING   172
Kenneth M. Reardon and Antonio Raciti

ACKNOWLEDGEMENTS   183

AUTHOR AND EDITOR NOTES   185

ABOUT SOCIAL POLICY PRESS AND ITS PUBLICATIONS   190

INTRODUCTION

First the backstory

A decade ago, the first venture for what has become Social Policy Press was launched with the publication of *Lessons from the Field: Organizing in Rural Communities* edited by Kristin and Joe Szakos. We had only been publishing the quarterly journal, *Social Policy,* for a couple of years at that point, gifted by Mike Miller, the veteran San Francisco-based community organizer and trainer. Joe approached us with an equally generous offer. If we would handle the layout, printing, distribution, marketing, and fulfillment, Kristin was a crackerjack editor and would do that piece, and his organization, named the Virginia Organizing Project at that point, would pay for the printing and leave us a couple of boxes left over for the sales. I knew Joe, first at Kentuckians For The Commonwealth (KFTC) and then at VOP and had long admired his work and that of both of these organizations, and furthermore part of my core commitment had always been that we all collectively owed a debt "to the field" of community organizing. Whenever we had a chance to pay off that debt, we had to do so. Besides, I had an essay on ACORN's famous Redfield Telephone Campaign that was to be included in the volume, so what the heck, let's ride.

Lessons from the Field: Organizing in Rural Comminities has never been what most publishers would call a best-seller, but borrowing a characteristic from the best of rural organizers and organizations, it has been steadfast and persistent. Hardly a month goes by when we don't sell a couple of books. Rarely does a new semester begin on some college campus or another in some pocket of America, more often than not along the byways rather than the big cities, that we don't see a spike in orders for this thin volume, clearly assigned by some professor or another, desperate to impart some other perspective on life—and struggle—in the countryside. At only 128 pages, it wasn't necessarily the mouse that roared, but it was squeaking along and clearly met a critical need.

A need that might continue to demand to be filled for organizers, activists, academics, students, and people who just plain want to see something done differently and want to do something about it. Noting the tenth anniversary of Joe and Kristin's *Lessons,* I reached out to them and asked how they would feel if we marked that anniversary by starting a series of *Lessons* books to see if such volumes could also bear up and meet similar needs in other areas: campaigns, actions, leadership development, research, politics, and so more. He of course agreed and volunteered to contribute, so away we went to try to bring this idea to reality.

The work order

Organizing continues to be a largely oral tradition. Organizers continue to largely be behind the scenes. When—and if—they write, it's more likely to be a leaflet than a case study, a memo rather than a *magnum opus*. Because so much of organizing is listening, they have a fine ear for what they are hearing. Most are more likely to tell war stories when they get together or at the back of the room, often about mistakes they made or amazing people and events they have witnessed, than they are to detail the nuts-and-bolts of their own work.

Nonetheless, we have recruited a wide number of deeply experienced community organizers to share the details of specific campaigns that open the hood and let anyone interested in going and doing likewise to see how they were built and driven. We gave everyone a simple outline of charges in writing about their organization's campaigns:

> Each essay should include the following:
> a. Background on the issue
> b. Background on the organization
> c. Staffing and leadership on the campaign
> d. Targets
> e. Demands
> f. Development and Timeline
> g. Actions
> h. Response and counter-response
> i. Negotiations (if any)
> j. Results
> k. Current status
> l. Lesson/s learned

I think you'll find that most of the following essays hit those marks—and more!

We did more than that in putting this book together. We looked through the last more than a dozen years of *Social Policy* editions to cull any case studies that we had printed previously and that still taught lessons that should be shared. Some of these were from organizers and others were from outside observers adding their unique and sometimes authoritative perspectives to campaigns as well. Some of the case studies seemed timeless and unique, others we updated when the campaigns seemed to be evergreen and enduring. If the campaigns demonstrated tactics and met the marks, we didn't care if they were from 1969 or 2017. Organizing and struggle are timeless, and all of our work is, and will continue to be, part of a proud and enduring tradition.

Of course, this isn't a "how-to" manual. Even the best and most committed readers won't be able to turn the corner of the pages and pretend this is a cookbook that if followed perfectly will lead to victories on every issue. The *a priori* that goes unsaid in almost every essay is the need to build some kind of organization or formation where people can act collectively, sometimes for years, to engage issues that are critical and persist until resolution.

Between these covers

This volume is about campaigns, but for the ease of the reader it is organized by various issues that these campaigns have addressed: jobs, income, housing, health, and so on. The issues that have ignited organizing campaigns are virtually infinite. Having organized for fifty years both domestically and globally, I have often joked that if any organization could create a replicable winning campaign to deal with loose dogs, bad sanitation, and sewerage and drainage issues, they could move the masses to topple the world. Yet, we don't have case studies on any of these three categories. There is always more to learn about issues and campaigns in working with people, and that is one element that makes community organizing so compelling—and necessary—for those of us for whom this has been our life's work and those of us who are facing a grievance that demands solution.

We start with "Jobs." Nik Belanger with Virginia Organizing details the successful effort to "ban the box." The box is the part of the job application that asks whether or not an applicant has had a felony or other conviction, and almost invariably discriminates not only against those that have run afoul of the law, but frequently by race as well. Lew Finfer, veteran and architect of many Boston-area organizations, shares how coalitions in Massachusetts skillfully utilized the initiative process to increase wages and develop grass-roots leadership and activism at the same time. Mike Miller shares the story of how the Mission Coalition Organization combined youth, tactics, targets, and political leverage to win jobs in this San Francisco community. If you had ever wondered, is there trouble in paradise, Drew Astolfi details how FACE launched a multi-year campaign in coalition with unions and other organizations to raise wages for home care workers and others in Hawaii.

In the "Income" section our contributors focus on campaigns driven by lower-income families and benefit recipients. Claire Gallagher provides an encompassing review of the hard fought "clawbacks" campaign in British Columbia by ACORN Canada where the members' creativity and persistence made an issue out of work-or-gift related income reducing (clawing back) benefit checks blocking claimants from ever getting even, much less ahead. The organization made the issue big enough that it broke the highest level of government in the province. I join the great labor and community organizer, Bill Pastreich, in sharing the basics of classic "minimum standards" campaigns that harken back to Fred Ross and the United Farm Workers, but were also staples of welfare rights organizing in both Brooklyn and throughout Massachusetts in the late 1960s. Having run those campaigns in Springfield, Boston, and elsewhere in that period, I have plied my trade with similar campaigns in Rome, Edinburgh, Belfast, Alaska, and the lower forty-eight for years whenever I could find the handle. In fact, ACORN's first campaign while we were still an affiliate of the National Welfare Rights Organization (NWRO) was modeled on the same principle. Steve Kest and I share the elements of that campaign from 1970-71 from Community Organizing Handbook #2. Judy Duncan, head organizer of ACORN Canada, recounts the long (now fifteen years and counting) fight of ACORN members there to block predatory lending and the starts and stops along the way in this struggle.

Campaigns around both access and the cost of health care are no stranger to mass-based community organizations. LeeAnn Hall shares the work done by Washington Citizen Action Network in pushing hospitals to rollback medical debt. Access and cost of ambulance service are not new issues. We share a case study written by Zach Polett from his experience with a unique campaign to win discounts for ambulance service for ACORN members in Fort Smith, Arkansas, in the mid-1970s.

Housing has consistently been a huge issue for community organizations composed of low-and-moderate income families, whether renters, prospective owners, or mortgage holders. John Anderson, ACORN Canada field director, and Marva Burnett, president of ACORN Canada, contribute an excellent analysis of the effort over a dozen years in Toronto to win landlord licensing for tenants of socially supported housing managed by private landlords, a campaign that began almost fifteen years ago and came to a culmination in 2017. Rent control has been at the top of the list for organizations fighting for affordable housing for tenants for decades. Davin Cardenas, co-director of the North Bay Organizing Project, headquartered in Santa Rosa, California, tells the story of winning rent control and then narrowly losing it in a referenda election after a withering campaign by real estate interests in a story that has not reached a final conclusion yet. One of the common issues for all tenants, especially public housing tenants, has always been the cost of services, like water and electricity. Adrien Roux, head organizer of the Alliance Citoyenne, ACORN's French affiliate, breaks down what it took to win the campaign to lower water bills in the social housing projects of Aubervilliers outside of Paris, the most low-income district in France. In the United States, arguably private housing tenants may have more protection and power in San Francisco than anywhere else in the country, and Randy Shaw, organizer and director of the Tenderloin Housing Clinic, explains why and the answer lies in the ability of organizations to come together to win Proposition H, it goes without saying, against the odds. In this section, David Tozzo, head organizer of ACORN Italia, provides a modern example of a minimum standards or benefit campaign, as he relates the back and forth swings of the pendulum for tenants winning lower rents by forcing their landlords to pay taxes.

Housing campaigns can also mean working to win access for families to financial products that allow them to own their own units. Unfortunately, for lower-income and working families that also may mean that they are targeted by companies using predatory products. The Great Recession of 2008 ushered back into many neighborhoods companies using contract deeds, rent-to-own, lease purchase options, and other schemes which might seem to pave a path to home ownership, but often were simply exploiting families in desperate need of housing with monthly payments that were cheaper than area rents. ACORN's Home Savers Campaign, launched in 2017 targeted—and won—with one of the largest players in this field. Dine' Butler, ACORN Home Savers program and research director, with me, as chief organizer, join to share our experience and that of the members and leaders.

Too often critics of community-based organizing from all sides of the political spectrum offer a rap against local group campaigns that they are all about stoplights, zebra crossings, and speed bumps. The essays in the section on Rights and Safety Campaigns for Women, Youth, and Immigrants are yet another reminder of how limited such understandings of organizing and how people see their issues really are. Beth Butler, longtime ACORN organizer and now director of A Community Voice, Louisiana ACORN's successor organization, and Ruth Rinehart, a former organizer and now Unitarian minister, write about hard and important campaigns by women and men in the organization to stop rape in the schools and win greater safety for women in Memphis, New Orleans, and elsewhere. Joe Szakos of Virginia Organizing shares the deliberate and methodical steps that the organization took in working with members who sought to win greater rights and acceptance of LGBTQ individuals in Charlottesville public schools. Emily Bloch outlines the campaign of the Merrimack Valley Project in Lawrence, Massachusetts, and the efforts of its immigrant members to win rights and protection regardless of their status in their communities.

Campaigns around City Services are indeed part of the bread-and-butter of many community organizations, but the taxes behind those services, though complex, are also a critical issue triggering many campaigns as well. The austerity regimes of the British government in recent years have meant massive cutbacks in financial support from the central government to the local city councils that provide local government. Nick Ballard, ACORN's head organizer in the United Kingdom, and Anny Crumble, former leader and now lead organizer for Bristol ACORN, share how they managed to turn back a council tax that would have hammered our members. "Leveling the Field: Winning Property Tax Equalization in Pulaski County, Arkansas" is an excerpt from a longer piece that Steve Kest and I wrote in the 1970s. "Don't be a Blockhead" by Professors Robert Fisher, Fred Brooks, and Dan Russell is an excellent external analysis of ACORN's campaign against H&R Block and its predatory Refund Anticipation Loan (RAL) program. This essay which we excerpted from *Let the People Decide* has become a standard in many academic circles as scholars and students have tried to understand community organizing campaigns. Equally instructive on the very local level might be the piece, again written by Steve and me, on winning the Centennial Park as part of the Save the City Campaign waged by ACORN in the early 1970s.

The first volume of the *Lessons from the Field* series focused on rural organizing, but certainly that doesn't mean that we shouldn't also include some case studies, both old and new, of major organizing campaigns in such an environment. Eloise Mallet of the French-based ReAct, Alliance, and ACORN's work in Africa, earlier had written in *Social Policy* about the multi-national campaign to force the transnational company Bollore-Socfin to deliver on its promises when they expropriated village lands for its palm oil and rubber plantations in Cameroon, the Ivory Coast, Liberia, Senegal, and Cambodia. She's updated the piece in this on-going fight for this volume. I dusted off an excerpt of an old piece that Steve Kest and I wrote on the campaign to stop the construction of Entergy's White Bluff plant. ACORN won half-a-loaf we might say, but there were many elements of the campaign that literally *made* the organization and its reputation making some of the lessons it provides timeless.

Finally, we come to development which too often has been what happens *to* community residents and their organizations rather than *with* them. We draw here on authors and organizers who have written in *Social Policy* in recent years about various organizing campaigns confronting developments whether stadiums, gentrification, or highways as well as the results of their efforts from negotiated community benefit agreements as well as the joys of victory and the pain of defeat. Gentrification seems everywhere and Dominic Moulden of ONE DC and Gregory Squires of George Washington

University offer their experience in the trenches updated to the current time. Randy Cunningham, an experienced tenant organizer and activist in Cleveland, documents the near victory in blocking the Q stadium there and its massive public subsidies and the sudden breakdown of their coalition with the negotiation of what Michael Powell, the "Sports of the Times" columnist in the *New York Times,* called a "sad agreement." We include here Darcy Pumphrey of Utah State's dissection of ACORN's campaign to modify and reroute what was called the Wilbur Mills Expressway in the 1970s and has now been built—to the worst of our predictions then—as the I-630 interchange. Professors Ken Reardon and Antonio Raciti write about the efforts of Foote Homes public housing tenants and their last stand to save public housing in Memphis from the wrecking ball that has swept cities around the country for the last more than thirty years.

These thirty essays don't tell all of the story of campaigns. Nothing ever could, but they continue the discussion and hopefully throw light on the path. There are no easy campaigns for community-based organizations, there are only degrees of difficulty. We win some, and we lose many. As long as community organizations are the vehicle for people to fight, then understanding as much about how campaigns are constructed and waged is essential. All the authors join in the commitment and hope that these essays improve the odds.

When I reached out to Steven Kest, the former executive director of ACORN, and told him I was going to include an excerpt he and I had written in 1977 on the campaign to stop the construction of Entergy's White Bluff coal-burning plant on the Arkansas River near Redfield, he replied, "I'm not sure that a 40+ year old essay stands as the last word in campaign strategy, but if you want to republish it that's fine with me." Of course, it's not the "last word," because peoples' organizing campaigns are going to always have to adapt to the times and conditions in which they are fought, but don't good soldiers study old battles to see what they can learn about winning new ones? Don't generals still dissect Valley Forge, Gettysburg, Custer's Last Stand, the struggles on the Maginot Line, the Battle of the Bulge, the Normandy Invasion, the Tet Offensive, and the disasters of Iraq and Afghanistan in order to learn something about what to do and what not to do? Believing good organizers do the same is part of the overarching spirit that propels this book. Hasta la Victoria!

UNDERSTANDING AND WAGING CAMPAIGNS
By Wade Rathke

Campaigns are moving trucks loaded with tons of issues

Campaigns are how organizations, leaders, and organizers drive issues from the privacy of personal dilemmas, kitchen conversations, and backroom laments onto the streets and from there to the public spaces where we can engage change. These trucks are always rolling, because there is never an end to the issues felt and faced by the powerless that demand expression and engagement by their organizations.

The list of issues is as broad as those covered in *Campaigns: Lessons from the Field*, except endless. Jobs, housing, income, health, security, development, and other issues that align with these essays are there, but so is education, police, race, disasters, and, as I have often pointed out, garbage pickup, sewerage and drainage, and loose dogs.

Not all issues become campaigns, but all campaigns are about issues

Saul Alinsky, the secular saint of community organizing, famously referred to the process by which issues evolve in their own survival of the fittest to actual campaigns is that issues needed to be "specific, immediate, and realizable." Yes, S.I.R, but it's more than that.

For an organization to take up a campaign, an issue has to be more than a problem, a good idea, or a policy prescription. It takes people willing to move it, to vote with their feet, as organizers say. Everything else being equal, no matter how good the issue might seem for a campaign or how winnable for the organization, if the organization can't translate the issue sufficiently for people to feel it deeply and be willing to fight for it, it's not going to emerge as a real campaign. Furthermore, as these essays show, without these deep commitments being felt by people for the issues and campaigns, the effort will not be sustainable for the years it can take to win. The examples are numerous from landlord licensing to land grabbing to predatory lending reforms and on and on and on as the authors in *Campaigns* articulate. An issue-based campaign is not just something where you add water and stir. For organizations, campaigns are commitments, waged until victory, no matter the time and trouble.

Campaigns come in all shapes and sizes and degrees of difficulty

The ten-cent, peanut gallery rap on community organizing campaigns has often been that campaigns are almost apolitical, speed bumps, zebra crossings, and stoplights. Certainly, among the old school "civics" and block clubs such issues were sometimes bread-and-butter, but a quick look at the table of contents of *Campaigns* puts the lie to these superficial claims. Campaigns range from very local issues like parks, stadiums, developments, and highways to power plant construction, federal and local taxes, and more. The other hard knock against organizing campaigns has usually been that, requiring community consensus and democratic approval, they were too middle-of-the-road and not edgy enough because organizers and leaders were unwilling to risk dividing their base. The evidence in *Campaigns* doesn't support that critique when you examine case studies about justice for felons in employment, welfare claimants over benefits, the rights of immigrants and the LGBTQ community, and safety and protection for women and rape victims.

Admittedly, modern community organizations are not your grandfather's notion of local group service projects. They have gone from being characterized by specific geographical boundaries to being welded together into multi-local, multi-state, even multi-national unitary or federated organization like ACORN to being networked together to give many community organizations in states or regions like PICO, Gamaliel, or even the IAF, the capacity to act in an extra-local manner on deeply grassroots issues. This is evidenced in the Blockhead case study on ACORN's campaign against H&R Block and other tax preparers' predatory refund anticipation loan (RAL) product in the United States or ACORN's fifteen-year slugfest against payday lenders in Canada.

Community organizations are also no longer an urban phenomenon in the barrios and ghettos of America. The campaigns of Virginia Organizing in small towns establish that there is no size bar or lack of fertile ground. The ACORN campaign against the White Bluff Power Plant and its organization of farmers on both sides of the Arkansas River to unite with other ACORN members in Pine Bluff and Little Rock who came to the issue from a consumer perspective rather than an environmental one makes a similar point, as do many of the case studies in *Campaigns: Lessons from the Field*. Nor are community organizations some version of American social change exceptionalism as the case studies from Canada, France, Italy, and Africa demonstrate.

Increasingly the repertoire of community organizations has changed dramatically as they have evolved past narrower geographical boundaries to become formations for popular action for diverse constituencies. In some cases, the structural boundaries of highways, hillsides, and waterways have still defined the catchment area allowing people to congregate, debate, decide, and act. In other ways organizations have become defined increasingly by their campaigns rather than any notion of geography. In many ways, community organizations have become the action arm of mutual interest networks. They are the human face and feet of human social networks, as opposed to those on the Internet. This evolution has allowed modern community organizations to continue adaptation and evolve as a strike force for social change at so many more levels.

In fact, in the way that campaigns define community organizations, organizers and leaders have sometimes found themselves struggling to maintain their multi-issued dimensions as their campaign muscle becomes more identifiable to the public and the press. ACORN in the United States went through many of these iterations where it was seen at different times as a welfare rights organization, a consumer organization, a tenant organization, a political organization, a workers' rights group when engaged in living wage campaigns, and sometimes people saw all of these faces simultaneously. In the same way Citizens in the United Kingdom is seen as a Living Wage organization or ACORN in the UK is seen as a tenants' union.

Members and other campaign participants don't seem confused about the modern community organization and their ability to engage various campaigns serially and simultaneously, but it is harder for others. Andrew Brietbart, the founder of the rightwing, conservative website, Breitbart.com, in the documentary "The Organizer" is seen in some footage telling Fox News that he thought "community organizing was helping Mrs. McGillicuddy bring in her trash," but in trying to understand ACORN he was confused about what community organizing was when he saw the organization doing campaigns to force banks to loan in lower-income neighborhoods and voter registration campaigns. He was OK with the former, and distinctly opposed the later. In the same documentary, Professor Francis Fox Piven, the renowned political scientist and theorist, in speaking of ACORN campaigns and organizing points out that ACORN's *modus operandi* "was a conflict model," rather than the classic social work and social service notion of community organization. Breitbart's nostalgia was clearly misplaced.

In the same way that there is no one type of organizing campaign, as the essays in *Campaigns* detail, there is also no one set of tactics that produce successful outcomes for members and adherents. In some cases, conflict on multi-fronts does lead to success. In other cases, eventual victories were the result of elaborate sequencing and engineering of ballot initiatives integrated with actions and other tactics as we see in the Proposition H campaign in San Francisco and the various living wage initiatives in Massachusetts and almost in the case of the Q Arena in Cleveland. In such situations, campaigns were advanced by integrating political capacity with organizational discipline, meetings, and actions.

Community organizations have gained remarkable dexterity as they have evolved. Still largely known for their "outside" game, they have also mastered the "inside" game, when needed and appropriate. The Charlottesville experience of Virginia Organizing was a master class in patience, leadership development, and behind the scenes organizing that understood that the potential for attack and division in conservative communities over LGBTQ rights argued for softer tactics like personal lobbying by the members that would pave the way for public action almost after victory was already assured.

All of which simply underlines the obvious emerging in virtually all of the essays in *Campaigns*. Tactics do not define campaigns, but campaigns in their various stages determine the tactics that will best advance their interests. An organization that always used any one tactic to advance a campaign would quickly find targets adjusting and absorbing the tactic. An organization that eschewed actions would be building walls that contained the anger and energy of its members. [A future volume in the *Lessons from the Field* series will examine tactics.]

Microsoft Word has a grammar and spellcheck feature that has become the crutch of millions. In reviewing and editing all of these pieces, Microsoft was continually annoyed and flummoxed by my unwillingness to make what they saw as the necessary modifications to the frequent use by our authors, particularly the organizers, of the expressions "take action" or "took action" in describing membership activity in a campaign. Microsoft instructed repeatedly that the proper expression would have not been "take action" but "act" and instead of "took action" would simply be "acted."

"Take action" speaks so distinctly to the common experience of community organizing campaigns because it accurately conveys the fact that action came out of an elaborate and extensive process. The weight of organizing, debate, decision, and only then finally "taking action" is so much richer than any simple expression or concept of action, but it speaks powerfully to the what is intrinsic about organizational campaigns.

If one of the criteria for a community organizing campaign is that the campaign must engage people to participate and act, many campaigns conducted by nonprofits and others are different. They are advocacy campaigns. Sometimes the issues that trigger them are the same, but the response is different. "Campaigner" is actually a job classification in many parts of the world based on a different "theory of change." The head of Aviz.org, the multi-million Internet campaign network, once described their theory of change to me. They would decide whether or not to embark on an Internet and petition-based campaign as determined by whether or not the "test" petitions returned enough response to indicate popular support. The same model prevails in principle on many social media campaigning formations which have become very popular including MoveOn.org, 38degrees in the UK, Leadnow in Canada, and GetUp! in Australia, among others.

Often, these campaigns are providing a valuable service of educating the wider citizenry about an issue or a potential threat. They share the essential organizational framing that positions an issue campaign as a moral right and imperative. They just serve different constituencies with a different methodology not reflected in the elaborate principles and practices of community organizations for whom "take action" signifies so much more. Certainly, community organizations also use social media "tools" and communications devices to advance their campaigns and to communicate and call their members and supporters into action as well. The fundamentally distinct accountability of the campaign within the organizing process starkly distinguishes the models. Advocates often have no discernible accountability mechanism that is equivalent to the leadership and participant process that is inherent in community organizing.

Campaigns also depend on "handles"

What's a handle? A way to grab the campaign might be the simplest definition. A handle for a minimum standard or benefit campaign, as Bill Pastreich and I describe in this volume, might be the process of listening on the doors and finding enough people who had gotten one thing or another from the welfare and discovering, as he did in Boston, that having several caseworkers verify the need and cost allowed the organization to campaign and win the benefit. Or, the handle might be equal protection under the law in such a case. In the Furniture of Families campaign in Arkansas, it was one vague line in a 400-page welfare manual that seemed to open the door to the campaign. In Italy, as David Tozzo describes, the language created by the Italian Senate in their bill to collect taxes from the black-market world of landlords and tenants was the handle that ACORN Italia was able to turn into a benefit campaign horrifying landlords and exhilarating the tenants who triggered the payments.

Though it was common to talk about handles fifty years ago, it is more common to hear much the same thing discussed as leverage now although they are significantly different. Handles were often found through the dialectic of discussions on the doors and painstaking research like that discussed in the White Bluff, Little Rock Property Tax, Bristol Council Taxes, Memphis public housing, and other campaigns. The requirement for an environmental impact statement was an example of a critical "handle" in the campaign against construction of I-630 in Little Rock. The contracts detailing promises made between Bollore and the villages before their land was grabbed were the handle on which that difficult campaign rested.

Leverage is something else, although a handle can be used to create leverage, it can also be something more. Leverage is the ability to move other actors into the campaign. Political scientist Michael

Lipsky famously described the way that organizational campaigns trigger other forces into the battlefield to intensify pressure on the targets of the campaign. A good example was the ability to move Harvard and other Ivy League shareholders of Entergy (Middle South Utilities then) to join ACORN in pressuring the company to reduce the size of its coal-fired plant. The use of referenda petitions in Santa Rosa in the attempt to force the council to live up to their rent control pledge was another. The same could be said of many living wage campaigns including the one detailed here from Massachusetts. Leverage can be a like a ricochet shot playing pool or billiards. An action on an indirect body that is more vulnerable to pressure or mass tactics that forces action by the primary target provides leverage. In Latin America and Africa, elections can provide leverage where normally government can be stubbornly unresponsive to popular demands and actions. The ability to cut off access to auctions for companies involved in various home ownership schemes with foreclosed properties provided the leverage to force the company to an agreement in ACORN's Home Savers Campaign.

In putting the tactics and strategy together to drive organizing campaigns, the search for handles and leverage is constant. No matter how we define the terms, these are essential ingredients and in dissecting almost any successful campaign, we can find them.

In looking at campaigns and how they work, we've come a long way from "specific, immediate, and realizable." Ideally, the lucky organizer might find these elements in whatever campaign the members and organizational participants determine to undertake, but sometimes the only thing certain when people raise their hands to vote is that the issue is felt painfully and personally by enough people that it can't be ignored. Frequently, as these essays reveal, the process of putting the campaign together involves breaking the issue down into pieces that can conform to the dynamics of a campaign. Parents, community members, and youth themselves may want jobs, but it would not necessarily have been enough for the Mission Coalition Organization in San Francisco to simply make signs and march down the streets demanding jobs to achieve what their campaign was able to muster. They needed to define the issue by selecting the targets and tailoring the demands to what they could win now in order to make the campaign "realizable." Similarly, the adjustments made in the Fort

Smith ambulance campaign reflect the way campaign demands adapt to reconcile community interests with real expectations.

Campaigns, like the decades long fights in Canada on payday lending and landlord licensing, are broken into pieces with short- and long-term objectives that allow for specific targeting and action to win some things like lower interest rates on loans or repairs by landlords in certain buildings, even while continuing to demand more comprehensive reforms. The real campaign, as we read in the case of Washington, DC, and ONE, is trying to win affordable and decent housing for existing residents. The stair stepping and scaling of campaigns towards such goals until they are achieved is one of the values of community organizations as opposed to ad hoc, advocacy, or social media campaigns. Organizing campaigns have a different level of persistence and sustainability fueled by the members and participants themselves that allows a longer staying power.

Campaigns don't forsake immediacy. Organizations know that they have to prove that collective activity works every day to deliver to their members or adherents in order to grow and win, but many of the benchmarks can be incremental as they are achieved as long as people are fully engaged and understand the campaign.

Organizing campaigns are sometimes derided as being too martial in their language and dynamics. What can I say? War and sports dominate the metaphors involving contentious struggle. Strategy, tactics, targets, "quick hits," strikes, actions are all vivid and expressive. Better language fails, but the power of the contest trumps the inadequacy of descriptions. Campaigns are about struggle, action and reaction, point and counterpoint, anticipation and response. Much is at stake, sometimes life and death, and almost always home and family, things that mean the world to people. Real campaigns are not artificial constructs to make a point or gain a mention in the press. They matter. It's serious. It's a battle where the sides are drawn.

As any description of campaigns also reveals, there are also winners and losers, or, as often as not, organizations winning less than they had demanded and losing less than had been at stake. Few victories are ever final in organizing. Opponents, better resourced, having more political clout, holding the fort, rather than storming it, rarely surrender and raise the white flag. They regroup, they lie in the weeds and wait. So, do we. Organizations and their opponents are often neither victors nor vanquished, as much as survivors. We never really lose until we stop fighting.

Nonetheless winning at whatever level is always better than losing because this involves people, not sport. Having been beaten back for years or having endured the issue endlessly, there's no such thing in our communities as building "more character," as the losing coach might say of his team. Organizations fight so hard because winning campaigns deeply felt and engaged by members and participants is not a game. It means something. It changes a part of the world we can impact. What was is now different. A new reality is created allowing new futures to become.

In the ebb and flow of these battles, the stories of campaigns sometimes veer into lawsuits or seek a peace in negotiations, neither of which was the objective of the campaign but each of which might have offered the possibility of settlement at least for a time. Housing, income, health, and the rest are not issues that any one campaign or even series of campaigns can "solve." Frequently, the heart of the organizational contribution is offering a vehicle for struggle, a way to keep fighting and carry on.

Organizers in my experience are often surprised that leaders and members value the fight more than the outcome. Many times, they never expected to win so their standards—and experience—differ in their expectations from the organizers. Being able to stand up and fight has a value in and of itself.

Organizers also judge the success—or failure—of a campaign in terms of whether it increases membership or the level of supporters and participants in the organization. No matter what the scorecard might be on any campaign, if the needle didn't move forward on these measures, it was not *a real organizing* campaign because it did not *build* the organization.

On this point there is a perfect alignment of all organizational interests between members, leaders, and organizers. The critical criteria of every campaign for all parties participating is whether or not it builds power for the organization and its people. Everyone understands that this is paramount, because there is always another fight coming.

In organizing, there is always another campaign.

BAN THE BOX IN SOUTHSIDE VIRGINIA
By Nik Belanger

JOBS

Across the United States, community organizations have been pressing local governments to adopt "ban the box" policies to remove questions about criminal history from public job applications. Designed to give returning citizens—people who have been incarcerated for felony or misdemeanor offenses—equal access to work by preventing employers from immediately filtering out all applicants with criminal records, "ban the box" requires that employers not ask about an applicant's criminal background until later in the hiring process.

When the city of Danville, Virginia, voted to "ban the box" in 2014, the process probably seemed straightforward to outside observers. A group of concerned citizens brought a good idea to city council, and city council recognized a good idea and voted unanimously to remove criminal history questions from city job applications.

But that's not really what happened.

To understand how Virginia Organizing—a grassroots organization with local chapters in all parts of the state—got a rural city in southern Virginia to adopt "ban the box", one must first understand the long process of community organizing that led to this victory.

In Danville, Virginia, unemployment has been higher than the state average for over a decade. A small city on the southern border with North Carolina, Danville struggles not only directly with serious economic issues but also with the effects of a local economy in decline. Population decline, substance abuse, homelessness, and increased incarceration have taken a high toll on the community.

It was under these circumstances that a small group of residents first formed the Danville chapter of Virginia Organizing. In the years before the Ban the Box victory, Virginia Organizing worked with some success to call for increased federal government spending on the creation of local public jobs and to promote a weatherization program to create jobs and lower utility bills for low-income renters.

Throughout this process, chapter leaders—in the beginning, a small group recruited through door-to-door canvassing and one-to-one conversations—worked together to build a diverse membership, form deep relationships across the city's many neighborhoods, and develop a political analysis of what needed to change in their city.

Beginning in 2012, Virginia Organizing held "restoration of rights" clinics in Southside Virginia. Virginia is one of only a few states that permanently disenfranchise citizens convicted of a felony, and only the governor can restore a citizen's right to vote. With training and support from the Advancement Project, leaders in the Danville and Martinsville/Henry County chapters learned how to navigate what was at the time a very complex process: different applications for different crimes, legal paperwork, reference letters, a personal essay, letters from local probation offices, and more.

At "restoration of rights" clinics, community members gathered together to learn about the restoration process and brainstorm ways to reach more returning citizens. Virginia Organizing held clinics in church basements, legal aid offices, public libraries, and other community spaces. A typical clinic included four types of people: facilitators, who had significant training and experience working on restoration of rights; leaders, who had some exposure to the process but lacked experience working on complex cases; allies, who were there to learn about restoration of rights for members of their church, clients of their nonprofits, or partner organizations; and new returning citizens, who came to start the process for themselves.

The local organizer and volunteer leaders recruited participants through intentional one-to-one conversations with a focus on asking people what issues mattered most to them and developing long-term relationships. By bringing this diverse group of people together, Virginia Organizing not only shared important information but also facilitated relationship building between community members who would not have otherwise found common interests.

While Virginia Organizing had a long history helping people get their rights restored and moving them to action in support of automatic restoration of rights, the process was new to many in Southside—and the demand for workshops, clinics, and one-on-one support was high.

Not only did dozens of people regain the ability to participate more fully in elections, but chapter leadership also expanded to include more people with direct, personal experience with the criminal justice system.

And voting booths were not the only place returning citizens faced discrimination.

Housing offices, social service agencies, and especially job lines were unwelcoming places for people with felony convictions on their records. After Anita Royston—whose youngest son had dealt with the struggle of life after incarceration—learned about what Virginia Organizing was doing and shared her story, a spark ignited the Danville chapter and one thing became clear: it was time to "ban the box" in the city of Danville.

Chapter leaders went about building relationships with other organizations in the area that addressed reentry issues. Barry Mayo, a case manager for a reentry program who worked out of the local community action agency, connected Virginia Organizing with a network of service providers, returning citizens, and probation officers. The network threw its full support behind the campaign.

It was through this network that Marty Jackson first heard about Virginia Organizing. A returning citizen who had spent nearly a decade in prison, Marty knew immediately that he wanted to be a part of making this change.

Despite the depth of their passion and steadfastness of their commitment, Anita, Barry, and Marty didn't do it alone. They attended Virginia Organizing meetings, shared their idea with leaders who had experience winning campaigns on different issues, and thought through what was needed to win this one. As Virginia Organizing built this campaign over the course of three months, leaders met with city councilors, reached out to the city's human resources department, researched existing ordinances in other Virginia cities, and spoke at community gatherings about this new idea spreading through the city.

Leaders also wrote letters to the editor and gave interviews to local media outlets. In meetings with Virginia Organizing leaders, five of the city's nine city councilors made commitments to vote in favor of removing questions about criminal history from initial job applications.

During the city council meeting when the ordinance was first introduced, dozens of supporters filled the city council chambers. Five supporters—Marty Jackson, Anita Royston, and Barry Mayo, joined by two pastors, Merri Davis and Joshua Hearne—shared their endorsements and personal stories with nine elected officials.

At the next city council meeting, two city council members spoke against the measure, raising doubts about its necessity and questioning its cost to the city; however, when the roll was called and votes were cast, the adoption of the ordinance was unanimous. Not only that, but members of city council looked to Virginia Organizing leaders for final approval of the ordinance's wording.

By meeting people where they are and working on the issues that matter to them, the Danville chapter of Virginia Organizing was able to win real change in the lives of real people.

And it didn't stop there: the same leaders who got involved through the Ban the Box campaign have led other winning campaigns. Along the way, they have grown as leaders, recruited new members, and worked to build strategic power with Virginia Organizing.

EQUITY FOR HOME-BASED CAREGIVERS IN HAWAII
By Drew Astolfi

From 2009 to 2014, Faith Action for Community Equity (FACE) Hawaii, a faith based organization with chapters on Oahu and Maui, reached the height of its power over its 20-year history. When we began our work in community organizing there was a lot of material about the deep listening and recognition fight stages. Of course building organization, developing leaders, and winning issues is what defines community organizing as different from other social change strategies.

Hawaii and FACE

FACE was founded by a set of clergy on Oahu in an attempt to respond to that challenge. They resolved to build an organization that would be rooted in faith values and would be able to champion the cause of the people who increasingly were being left out of the economy and government of the state.

FACE took on a set of jobs issues in its early years including a hard fought, but ultimately failing effort to pass a living wage ordinance in Honolulu. "Jobs was a hard issue for FACE, we kept losing. We lost a living wage bill at the City Council two years in a row, we lost our subsequent effort to pass a first source hiring law, but things kind of turned around for us when we discovered by accident, or maybe by providence, the idea of a sectoral strategy. This happened during the Hotel Workers Rising contract negotiations in 2005 and 2006," said Rev. Stan Bain, chair of the Jobs Committee during that time.

The Hotel Workers Rising campaign in 2005-06 was a nationwide contract fight between UNITE HERE locals and the big hotel of chains in ten cities including Honolulu. The effort was aimed at improving an entire sector, the economy of hotel work, especially housekeeping. UNITE HERE's Hawaii chapter, Local 5, is FACE's sole union member and FACE actions supported the effort.

"Hotel Workers Rising moved our leadership to a new understanding of local economics and how a group could intervene in a local economy. ...we'd always been clear on the theological imperative to improve the life of workers, but this idea of a jobs sector fired our imagination in more secular terms," said Dr. Jon Davidann, an historian at Hawaii Pacific University who helped lead the Jobs Committee work over many years. For UNITE HERE, tens of thousands of hotel workers benefited; for FACE it gave us the confidence to lead the organization into a deeper economic justice campaign based on a sector. And the obvious sector for FACE to focus on was home health care.

Home health care—fastest growing jobs sector in Hawaii

In late 2010 FACE voted to work on a multi-year sectoral jobs strategy focused on improving home health care jobs. Like many faith-based community organizations, FACE broke the calendar year into three parts: a base building and listening trimester that ran September to December, followed by an action and accountability campaign trimester from January to June, and ending with a celebratory and fundraising trimester from June to August. FACE had a weighted voting system to decide which issues to work on, and usually ended up with three or four issues coming to the fore, leaving some groups of leaders frustrated.

Choosing home health care as a priority issue knit two of our most important issue committees together, jobs and health care. Merging the committees worked because the Health Care Committee was already working on long-term care. On the consumer side the committee had helped propose, along with AARP and the Longshoreman's retiree club, a state funded study looking at the viability of creating the nation's first state sponsored long-term care insurance. On the Jobs Committee side FACE had cut an early issue by creating a training program for Tongan women working in home health care to become Certified Nursing Assistants (CNAs) and raise their pay.

FACE had a significant base of leaders and supporters in the Tongan community in Hawaii, and many Tongans held key leadership positions in the organization. Tongans are a more recent group of immigrants to Hawaii, coming in large numbers in the 1970's. Tongan culture, like many Polynesian cultures, places a high value on elders and care for the aging. Care work is a position of importance and respect among Tongans and many of them gravitated to home health care work in Hawaii. Reverend Ane Aholelei of Kilohana UMC explained, "It's important to us to care for aging people, and we are strong and kind…it's good work to do and we like to do it, in fact it is a blessing to do it, but," she added, "we really wish it paid better. It's a sign of the way American society values elders that it pays so poorly."

There were ultimately three strategic factors for picking home health care as an issue. First it affected a lot of FACE members, both workers and consumers. So the issue built the organization's base of leadership directly. Moreover, at that time home health care was the fastest growing jobs sector of the state's economy. The work was poorly paid and mostly unregulated, existing outside the normal workplace protections.

Most importantly for FACE, the issue mobilized deeply held values. "This is about the relationships that matter most to us, parents and children, at a time when they need the most from us," explained FACE Oahu Lead Organizer Patrick Zukemura. "A faith based organization (needs) to select issues that lend themselves to a clear values frame because this is how faith based community organizing contributes to building each church or temple's ongoing vision of how they are living out the strictures of their faith. This is the symbiosis of justice and worship. When we do this correctly, we tap a very strong current in people, and that is what changes things in Hawaii."

It's worth noting that the decision to create a sectoral strategy for our jobs work was not the deeply analytical "chess master" approach that is valued so highly among think tanks and philanthropic foundations. FACE leadership had a solid understanding of the current conditions but we also had to make guesses about the future because there is no perfect strategy chart leading from one discrete stage of this intervention to the next. Community-driven policy does not work that way. We were clear that there were stages to the work and the first stage was credentialing the organization's ability to deliver improvements to the base of women who were the heart of care work. We knew it was only after we'd made progress on this first stage that we could expect to take on larger issues.

Credentialing FACE's work in the sector: 2010 to 2013

FACE began its multi-year intervention with a series of incremental fights that were selected by the women working in home-based care who attended our churches with help from some of the consumers. To get this right, FACE staff and leaders conducted deep listening in the set of member institutions closest to the consumers and workers.

For example, we held three listening sessions over two months at Kilohana Methodist Church on the windward side of Oahu. More than sixty women participated, mostly Tongan, who were currently working as CNAs or who had previously worked as CNAs but stopped because of the barriers to keeping their certification. About a dozen of these women brought their daughters with them.

These listening sessions were hours long and identified a laundry list of specific barriers to earning a living as a home health care worker. First, the training required for certification is costly and did not allow for a translator to assist with the medical vocabulary used during the training. Once certified, that certification is good for only two years and then there is a process for re-certification which is cheaper and does not require additional training, as long as each applicant for recertification could prove that they had worked in a certified home care facility for at least eight hours during the past two years. But our members did not work in a care facility, they worked as contractors in patients' homes. This requirement of eight hours in a home care facility meant that CNAs in Hawaii who worked in patient's homes, while fully trained and certified, were forced to start from scratch with the full cost of training (between $900 and $2,000) every two years.

Another barrier for our members was that as they were contractors, the agencies who hired them did not pay any benefits. These women worked their physically demanding jobs without workers compensation, medical insurance, disability insurance, or sick leave. All of the women had stories of major injuries from the heavy lifting required by the job and also related dangers like dogs on the property or poor conditions in and around the patients' houses. The state's refusal to allow translators for the written portion of the driver's test or to offer translated written tests also limited their ability to get car insurance and have dependable transportation to care for their patients.

They were also frustrated that the agencies they worked for charged four and five times more for their work than the women were paid. If fact, most of the women were not paid mileage or for the time it took them to drive from patient to patient. Exasperated, one of the women said, "Why can't we be the bosses and the carers? Then we could make sure the patients and the carers are all taken care of." This phrase was repeated often as the campaign went on.

Finally, the women were also worried about the patients who needed care but could not afford trained caregivers. FACE already had experience running the CNA certification training with the help of Dr. Ceria-Ulep, chair of the University of Hawaii School of Nursing (now the Assistant Dean). Dr. Ceria-Ulep coordinated resources for free training for large classes of women, allowing the time for a translator to help with the medical terminology when necessary.

For the women who already had CNA certification, we decided to challenge the eight-hour requirement. We couldn't find the eight-hour requirement in the law, so we met with the state's Workforce Development Director, James Hardaway. Hardaway agreed that the eight-hour requirement was a barrier for thousands of home care workers across the state. Then we met with State Senator Roz Baker, the chair of the powerful Consumer, Commerce, and Health Committee in the Senate. For years Senator Baker had been an advocate for families to have the opportunity to care for elders in their own homes. Senator Baker figured out that the eight-hour requirement was not in the law, but had become the interpretation of the law. She made calls for us during an afternoon meeting confirming this and making plans to fix the problem. Within a week, we had a letter from the state waiving the eight-hour requirement as long as the re-certification applicants followed the rest of the required application process.

At the same time as these FACE leaders were eliminating this barrier, the state of Hawaii decided to contract with an out-of-state testing company, replacing the Red Cross which had run the process for years. With the new testing contractor came new forms for re-certification and those new forms required proof of eight-hours working in a care facility. The women tried for weeks to talk with the new company but they hadn't opened an office yet in Hawaii and the call center staff who answered the toll-free number had no idea how to answer the women.

Finally, we heard an office was opening on Oahu so a dozen of the women carpooled to the new office. The office was so new that that there was no furniture or staff yet, but there was a woman setting up the phone system who talked with us. She had no idea how to address our issue but she gave us the name of the owner of the company who ultimately agreed to help. His staff figured out how our applicants could modify the application for re-certification and our members starting getting re-certified without having to start over with all of the training again. This improvement helped establish FACE as a force for care workers, not just because it saved thousands of home health care workers thousands of dollars across the state but also because it was the first time that the home care system in Hawaii acknowledged the role of non-facility based home care workers.

Domestic Workers' Bill of Rights/Meeting Caring Across Generations 2013

Meeting Ai-Jen Poo of the National Domestic Worker Alliance was a turning point in FACE's work on these issues. Hawaii's First Lady at the time, Nancie Carraway, created a monthly salon to "elevate the political discourse" and she invited leaders from FACE to the governor's mansion to meet Ai-Jen and consider ways to improve conditions for domestic workers. Carraway and Poo proposed creating a domestic workers' bill of rights. Following the salon, the bill had the full-throated support of the governor and moved quickly through the state legislature. The governor signed the Domestic Workers' Bill of Rights and it was the first piece of legislation the governor signed that year.

While not a product of FACE's sectoral work or a part of our initial plan, the victory was a windfall for the campaign. Our contribution to the effort was not to project power since Governor Neil Abercrombie provided that, but rather to provide stories from our home health care workers that informed both the regulations and implementation of the law. Our success in working on this led Poo to invite FACE to join a joint effort called Caring Across Generations that she was building with Sarita Gupta of Jobs with Justice. They were interested in the work FACE was doing on long-term care, as well as the direct work we were doing with caregivers. This was dramatically helpful when the organization began to focus on creating a new state benefit program to promote aging in place.

Importantly for our work we ensured that the law included iron-clad provisions to cover home health care aides under the state minimum wage law. This mattered because we had begun an effort to increase wages and was a precondition for FACE's successful minimum wage campaign. Once the bill became law, First Lady Caraway appointed FACE staff Veronica Geronimo to help set up the administration of the law. While the bill passed on the star power of Nancy Caraway and Ai-Jen Poo, we were able to bring care workers into the room, and help focus the state labor department on where and how to publicize the law.

Building on success 2014–2017

By the end of 2013 the leaders of jobs/health care sectoral strategy had become central leaders of FACE on both islands. While substantial improvements had been made at the edges of the working conditions of caregivers, we wanted fundamentally to meet Reverend Ane Aholelei's challenge to raise the women's wages. With the Domestic Workers' Bill, certification training costs and re-certification barriers were behind us and we were more willing to take risks.

We decided to aim our work at both a broad wage increase for everyone by raising the minimum wage and a deep wage increase by creating a worker-owned cooperative that would symbolically challenge the agency driven model of home health care delivery.

According to Leotele Togafau, who began working with FACE as a volunteer while she was staff to Local 5 and lead staff for the minimum wage effort, "We knew we needed a new wage floor for the workers but to solve that problem we needed to enlarge it, and raise up everyone, that's why we took on minimum wage."

In 2013, FACE, ILWU, Appleseed, Pride at Work, UNITE HERE, the social service coalition PHOCUSED, and the Hawaii AFL-CIO made a late run at raising the minimum wage and while the bill had gone further than we expected it to, it ultimately failed. We'd done this in preparation for a bigger effort in 2014 because it often took two sessions to make or change a law.

While the initial plan for 2014 was to ask for $9.50 an hour, and pre-session work in the fall of 2013 produced a $9.50 bill, we were forced to change it when Obama's state of the union speech in 2014 had our legislative champions, FACE leaders, and union activists scrambling to change the bill to $10.10 per hour. Senator Clayton Hee, the Senate sponsor and fierce champion of native Hawaiian issues called us right after the Obama speech laughing, "so now it's $10.10, eh? Don't want to look bad in front of our President, right?" He rewrote the bill overnight and replaced our original $9.50 per hour version with $10.10 per hour right away, but the House version that moved was only $10.

While FACE helped lead a large labor/community coalition, most of the ground troops for passage of the increase were care workers activated in the earlier jobs sector issues. The Restaurant Association, the state Chamber of Commerce, and the Food and Beveridge Association were initially actively opposed. In the early debates in the House and Senate, this opposition made a common argument: that the people who got minimum wage were all young students and part-time workers. This had been the argument that brought down the effort to increase the wage in 2013.

The opposition argument was shattered by the dozens of care workers who showed up in large numbers midway through the session to humbly ask for a raise. Tiala Toetu'u, an important voice in the Tonagan community in Hawaii, spoke at the March crossover House hearing in the Finance Committee—the same committee that had killed the bill in the previous year. She said, "But we are not students and we are not young, we are grown women, we take care of your parents, we help your families, and we are blessed to do it. But we get paid very little and these islands are very expensive. Please don't be confused by who we really are when you vote on this…" Backed by twenty-four Tongan women dressed in ta'voala skirts, dressed "as if we were going to church", they effectively silenced the restaurant lobby and the House bill successfully crossed over to the Senate.

After that hearing, the opposition to the bill split. Sherry Menor, the director of the state Chamber of Commerce and the sister of a Honolulu City Councilor, who was FACE's most prominent housing ally, shifted the Chamber's position and began to argue that there was in fact a need for a minimum wage increase, especially for "the caregiver women." With the Chamber's mild support, the dynamic around the issue changed. The effort still took several additional mobilizations, including a concert and rally inside the state capitol rotunda and leaders running around with Senator Hee taping dimes to legislators' desks to pressure the House members to accede to the additional 10 cents in the Senate bill. The session ended with the Governor signing the $10.10 per hour bill into law with better provision for tipped workers. At the signing, State Labor Director Dwight Takamine, who had helped write the rules for the Domestic Workers' Bill of Rights and had been a resolute supporter of the effort to raise the minimum wage, elbowed Tiala Toetu'u saying, "Now let's work on that co-op idea of yours!"

Building the Kilohana Angels Cooperative

Even during the excitement of passing the minimum wage, there was a sense that this was not going to be enough to challenge the way the system of care work was delivered to people aging in place. The FACE caregivers had contracts at agencies that often charged the families via insurance or Medicaid between $40 and $58 an hour, while the workers made minimum wage or a little higher. Addressing this inequity meant adjusting the industry itself.

Figuring out how to "be the bosses and the carers, so that the patients and the carers were taken care of" required more than simply the change of a law. After months of research and conference calls with experts across the country including the long running Cooperative Health Care Associates in the Bronx, the women decided to become a worker-owned cooperative. By this time Senior Minister Reverend Mark at Kilohana Methodist had retired but that just meant he had more time to help the women develop their business plan. There was no one on the islands to look to for advice: this would be the only worker-owned home care cooperative in Hawaii. They made it work. Kilohana Angels registered with the State in March 2014, and funded their business plan in a single night by inviting the public to a traditional Tongan Calabash fundraising dance.

KupunaCare 2015–2017

The last issue FACE took on during its sectoral jobs intervention was an effort to create the nation's first state-funded long-term care reimbursement program. The effort, ultimately called KupunaCare (Kupuna is Hawaiian for respected elder) pays $70 a day for long-term care services. All Hawaii citizens could tap this to support their elders aging-in-place once they needed an advanced level of care,

and it included reimbursing costs to hire caregivers in your home. FACE had almost won this issue in 2002, passing it in the House and Senate, but it was defeated by a veto from the first Republican Governor in Hawaii since right after statehood.

With the assistance of Caring Across Generations, and help from the Hawaii AARP and our allies in the ILWU, we brought the issue back to the legislature in 2016 and again in 2017. There was a strong effort to kill the bill early in 2016. Newly ascendant conservative forces in the state were particularly opposed. FACE needed a show of force to drive the bill to be reintroduced in 2017. Leadership rallied and held a large accountability session at Sacred Hearts' with hundreds of lay people from the FACE churches. Despite the tough first year the bill did pass in 2017, in part as a result the inspired leadership of Pedro Haro-Siurno, a young health care activist hired by Caring Across Generations to push the bill at the legislature. By 2017 the FACE's focus had passed from the sectoral jobs campaign but FACE job leaders like Clementina Ceria Ulep, retired staff Patrick Zukemura, and Tiala Toetu'u stayed on the issue until the bill was signed by Governor David Ige. These leaders are active today in writing and revising work rules for the state Department of Labor that govern elements of the home care profession.

What was out of our reach

Two hoped-for changes that seemed reasonable when FACE laid out its initial strategy of community-driven reform of the home health care sector remained just out of reach for us. First, we had hoped to unionize the workforce. Hawaii is a strongly pro-union state and has the second highest rate of unionization of any state in the US. While both AFSCME and SEIU are successful in unionizing these workers in other states, each union faced obstacles to organizing these workers in Hawaii. In the end unionization was beyond the reach of our effort.

Second, we considered the creation of a mutual aid society that purchased workers compensation insurance for it members. We thought this would allow us to organize much larger numbers of CNA's into an institution, since it required a large number of purchasers to function. If successful it would have afforded us access to very large numbers of workers. But the startup costs were high, and we abandoned the idea as beyond FACE's means after a brief business plan and a handful of meetings with insurance companies.

FACE was able to successfully conclude this seven-year sectoral strategy because we were able to hold enough power to win each of the individual issue campaigns while always placing each issue campaign in the larger narrative around home care as a sector that must be fundamentally improved for both workers and consumers. The changes in certification rules and costs are the roots of the nation's first state funded universal long-term care benefit plan and one of the higher state minimum wage structures in the US.

WINNING WAGE INCREASES USING REFERENDA IN ORGANIZING
By Lew Finfer

Background
Twenty-six states allow some kind of referenda. These are forms of direct democracy where the voters decide on passing laws. Often a Governor, House Speaker, Senate President, or political party can prevent a law from passing or water it down because of the power of their office and control of the legislative process. Too often it is the big business groups who have the access and power to persuade politicians.

Referenda enable another possibility by allowing community, labor, and religious groups to bring something to all the voters. We remember family gatherings where there's a kids' table and an adult table. In public life, the community, labor, and religious groups are at the kids' table and the political and business leaders are at the adult table. But with signature-gathering followed by voter education and turnout to bring referenda to the ballot and win them, we can get to the adult table and start making policy ourselves.

In 2012, the Coalition for Our Communities campaigned in Massachusetts for new tax revenue through a progressive tax package. The House Speaker and Senate President said no, and that was the end of that; they had the power to block it.

So, in 2013, when a new community, labor, and religious-based coalition called Raise Up Massachusetts was formed, we started with the idea of taking something to the ballot by referendum rather than another legislative campaign. We collected 390,000 signatures over the required two periods during 2013-2014 to qualify raising the minimum wage from $8 to $11 an hour and for an earned sick time law. Because the legislature believed our minimum wage initiative would pass at the ballot, they passed it legislatively just before our deadline for turning in the signatures. To ensure we didn't take it to the ballot, despite it not including all our provisions, they even raised the wage to $11 an hour! On the other hand, they refused to take up earned sick time, so we filed the signatures and organized and won the ballot vote by 59 percent to 41 percent.

Ingredients of a successful campaign

Of course, you need a strong coalition capable of collecting hundreds of thousands of voter signatures and then doing the voter education and turnout work to win at the ballot. A decent budget is needed to have some staff, some polling, and some ability to buy paid media.

Signature gathering was the glue to our power and accountability. If you get the signatures, you move forward; if you don't, you're dead. We asked each participating organization to set a signature-collection goal and each week a report was circulated showing how many signatures every organization had reported to date. Each group knew how hard they had to work to organize volunteers to collect the signatures in front of stores, at meetings, at public events, after religious services. When they saw the other groups in the coalition meeting their goals, they got motivated to fulfill their own, and we knew we had a strong and accountable coalition.

Campaign 2017-2018

Our 2017-2018 campaign prioritized two referenda: one to raise the minimum wage to $15 an hour (the "Fight for $15!") and the other to create a paid family and medical leave program—to enable paid time off for new parents or a serious illness or injury. Additionally, through a parallel process, we were trying to pass a constitutional amendment for an additional tax on incomes over $1 million to fund education and transportation.

We collected a total of 360,000 signatures required for the two referenda in the fall of 2017 and spring of 2018. We had seven regional accountability meetings with legislators to get commitments to pass these legislatively as well. We had phone banks using the "magical" predictive dialer that allows a volunteer caller to reach twelve or more actual voters an hour by phone. And we had a statewide rally of 800 activists at our state capital. Of course, we didn't neglect social media either.

Unlike in 2013-2014, this time big business groups didn't let us have the playing field of referenda all to ourselves. The Retailers Association of Massachusetts collected signatures to cut the sales tax by $1.2 billion. They didn't so much want to win that as to use it as leverage to get a two-day annual sales tax holiday and an end to a law enabling retail workers to be paid at time and a half for work on Sundays and holidays.

The House Speaker and Senate President asked Raise Up and the big business groups to meet together with legislators to negotiate passing these as laws instead of going to the ballot. Negotiations went on between a six-member Raise Up negotiating team, six representatives from five major big business groups, and six members of legislative leadership. Negotiations went on over six weeks, but then the legislators wrote their own compromise bill.

Things were up-ended in part when our state Supreme Court ruled the Millionaires Tax off the ballot in a suit brought by five major big business organizations (only partly overlapping with the ones in the negotiations on the other issues). The decision turned on an interpretation of what constituted unrelated items in a ballot proposal with a majority of judges saying raising taxes on millionaires and spending it on education and transportation were unrelated. In the 5 to 2 decision against us, five of the judges had been appointed by first term Republican Governor Charlie Baker (who was able to appoint so many because the others had reached their retirement age).

This led to the legislators deciding to offer a proposal to raise the minimum wage to $15 over five years and to pass a strong paid family medical leave law. But fearing that the Retailers sales tax referendum might win (despite our pledge to fight it at the ballot), they gave them a five-year phase-out of Sunday time and a half pay and a smaller tipped wage increase if they withdrew their referendum, which they did. On our side, we were able to prevent a teen sub-minimum wage proposal from being added to this deal.

Raise Up Massachusetts has an eleven member Steering Committee of community, labor, and religious groups. Labor groups provide most of the money for the coalition, but on the key organizing work of signature-gathering, the community, labor, and religious groups generally collect one third of the signatures each. We also have a broader body in the Raise Up Coalition called the Grassroots Committee where all participating groups make decisions on what our issues will be and major strategy issues like moving them to the ballot or accepting a legislative compromise proposal.

We voted not to go to the ballot on paid family medical leave because the legislation offered was close enough to what was in our ballot proposal for it to be a major victory. We voted not to go to the ballot on minimum wage because we achieved our main goal of raising wages for 840,000 low-wage workers by $2.75 billion in wage increases. Even had we gone to the ballot, we could not have stopped the cut in Sunday time and a half pay for retail workers because that was not part of the minimum wage law. The lower raise for tipped workers was at least partially offset by our defeat of the proposal for a sub-minimum wage for teens.

Lessons learned

Referendum campaigns are tremendous opportunities for leadership development since many thousands can concretely contribute by volunteering to gather signatures. Large turnouts at accountability meetings with public and private officials (one of our top tactics to be sure) are still only organized by scores of volunteer leaders, whereas signature gathering campaigns need many thousands to step up.

When developing a referendum, careful legal research is needed to try to ensure what's proposed cannot be challenged successfully in court.

Polling is not the final word, but it helps us find out what people find compelling, and what arguments are more persuasive than others. It's a crucial tool along with our own political common sense to shape what our proposals should be.

We need to try to anticipate what big business groups will do in directly opposing our referenda with arguments and money spent against it. We need to anticipate what ballot proposals they might file that in and of themselves are harmful to people or can be tools to undermine what we are proposing.

Accountability builds power. Making collective decisions and setting goals and reporting on signature-gathering, number of phone calls made, number of homes canvassed, and number of people attending meetings with legislators are the key to our power and emphasize the need for mutual accountability to meet the goals each organization pledges to.

Relationship-building among coalition members is important so we can be a team and not a committee doing a task. That can be fostered by doing 1:1's during meetings, outside of meetings, and by relational-rounds meetings. There are different cultures in labor unions, community groups, and religious organizations that can create tensions that are best overcome when there are strong personal relationships between participating leaders and organizers, mutual respect, and accountability. This is hard to do when there's a lot of work to do and people want to get the tasks done. Balancing tasks with relationship-building is a tension in organizing.

In many blue states, Democratic legislators still see themselves as negotiating between what big business wants and what community, labor, and religious groups want. In red states, legislators work hand in hand with big business groups for their agenda. Only if more legislators are elected or challenged based on their positions on issues will this picture change.

Writing new stories

Organizer Larry McNeil develops a theme in his essay "Congregations for a New Millennium" for what transformative organizing does. It allows people to tell their stories about the pain of the lack of opportunity and discrimination they experience. Then by reflecting on those stories, and acting together—as our democratic and Biblical faith traditions call on us to do—we can make sure more hopeful stories can be told. Simply put: tell our stories, reflect on our stories, write new stories.

I remember the stories of women who had to go back to work way too soon after their child was born or the anguish of not having been able to take off work to be with a seriously ill spouse because they lacked paid leave time. Now with a strong paid family medical leave law, there will be new stories with less pain as people have this wonderful benefit to give them deeper security in their lives. A $15 minimum wage that was once dismissed as nice but unreachable, is now the law in our state, as well as in California and New York, Seattle and Washington, DC, and hopefully in more places sooner than later. Those better wages are about dignity and being able to do something more for yourself and your family.

SUMMER JOBS FOR YOUTH: The Mission Coalition Organization Campaign
By Mike Miller

In the Fall of 1968, 800 delegates and alternates from more than sixty member organizations attended the founding convention of a multi-issue, mass-based, predominantly Latino coalition in the Mission district of San Francisco called the Mission Coalition Organization (MCO).

In the first year, youth leaders and some adult (mostly teacher) allies planned, and then in early 1970 waged, a campaign that won about 200 part-time summer youth jobs.

I was MCO's lead organizer, and staffed the Jobs Committee.

That summer, jobs were at a premium. The Neighborhood Youth Corps, part of President Lyndon B. Johnson's war on poverty program, didn't offer enough of them. MCO approached large companies with facilities in the Mission district and proposed that they create summer jobs for neighborhood youth. Young people could stand in for workers taking summer vacation or do delayed clean-up or other tasks in a company's facilities.

The large Wonder Bread/Hostess Cupcakes neighborhood production plant was first. Jobs Committee Chair Larry Del Carlo called and got an appointment with plant superintendent Norman Steinke. On the appointed day, a call from the company's secretary told us, "The appointment is cancelled." No other date was offered.

The dozen or so of us who would have been the disciplined negotiating committee huddled, determined this was not acceptable, and agreed we would go to the company building, march in, and stage a sit-down in the office. We did. Larry Del Carlo blocked Steinke's access to his phone, but Steinke indicated through a large glass window to his staff that they shouldn't call the cops. For two hours, in a room getting smokier and smokier, (this was long before "no smoking") with tensions rising, we were deadlocked.

Lesson: Our broad base of membership gave us legitimacy, as did support from the Joint Strategy and Action Committee (JSAC) of the Northern California Council of Churches. We later learned that Steinke was a Methodist, and talked about MCO with his minister

who called Rev. Robert Davidson, JSAC's Executive Director, and learned we were a credible group.

Lesson: In those days, nonviolent direct action was widely regarded as a legitimate tactic. In a different time, we might have ended up in jail.

Lesson: Luck isn't something you can count on; we had it. Had we been arrested the organization probably would have split. Our moderates would have quit.

Steinke broke the impasse, saying he would meet, if we left. "Why should we trust you?" we asked. "You've made your point," said Steinke, "I'll do it; you've got a bunch of witnesses." That wasn't enough. He agreed to put it on paper, and sign. That was sufficient.

Lesson: You've got to know when you've won, and act accordingly; just as you have to know when to fight. We knew.

On the appointed day, we met with Steinke. Our spokesperson proposed ten jobs; the company countered with four. At one point, Steinke said he couldn't agree because these were union jobs. We told him, "We spoke with Labor Council Secretary-Treasurer Jack Crowley and this is o.k. with him as long as union wages are paid." The negotiation moved on.

More back-and-forth got us to six, and we agreed. We then pulled from our hip pocket our joker in the deck; divide the jobs in thirds so that through the course of the summer three kids can work. (Their pay would equal that of a full summer NYC job.) A deal was struck.

Lesson: Expect divide-and-conquer in one of its multitudinous manifestations. Cut the possibility off at the pass by discussing with organized labor any plan you have for jobs; get their approval. Pause along the way to get it, if you have to. MCO did this with the building trades on Model Cities. The Building Trades Council demanded one-third of the Model Cities planning body's board seats. MCO said "No". Joe Mazzola, Plumber's Union president, and Dan Del Carlo (no relation to Larry), council secretary-treasurer, insisted. On a pre-arranged signal, I tugged at MCO President Ben Martinez' sleeve and said, "This isn't going anyplace, Ben, let's go." We got up to leave. "Sit down, sit down," said Mazzola, "We're going to work this thing out here." We did.

Lesson: If you have power, act or threaten to act.

Our team returned to MCO headquarters to discuss allocation of the jobs. I was dismayed to see the committee turn itself into a social welfare agency. The conversation went something like this:

Q: Who's going to get the jobs?

A: Kids who need them.

Q: How are we going to know who needs them?

A: They'll fill out an application, and there will be a statement of need.

Q: What if they lie?

A: We'll have to have a way to check.

Members Ventura Martinez, Elba Montes, Luisa Ezquerro, Ena Aguirre Spackman, Juanita, Joe, Larry and Joan Del Carlo (mom, dad, son, and daughter), Fernando Cosio, Rich and Kathy Loos, Jim Donton, and others got into the details. Heated discussion ensued.

At one point, previously quiet Joan Del Carlo said, "Why don't we give the jobs to the people who participate in getting them?" Sudden silence. Everyone in the room knew the wisdom of the idea. A point system emerged as the mechanism to implement it: a point

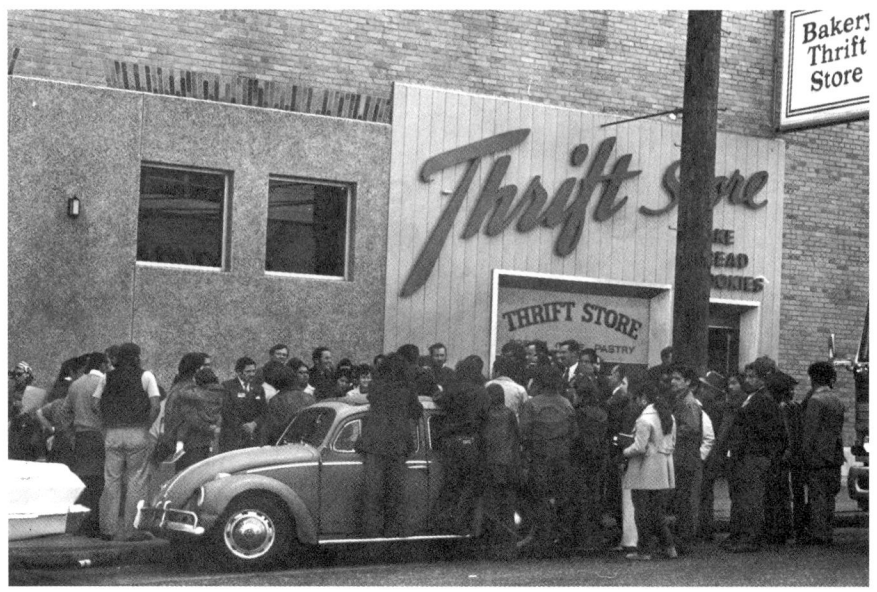

for coming to a meeting, a negotiation, or an action. The person with the most points got first crack at a job. S/he could take it, refer it (and lose accumulated points), or "pass"—keeping his/her points, and wait for the next job. The committee came to be called "The Beast" as members sought new negotiations and actions to gain points.

Lesson: MCO almost transformed itself from a membership organization to a provider-client agency. Had we become that, it would have undermined the idea of membership. We would have been co-opted by our own doing—as the whole housing movement of that period was largely co-opted by housing and community development corporations. A brilliant insight by a young member saved MCO's jobs campaign. The point system carried over into the fall effort for adult, full-time jobs. By late fall, 300 people were attending weekly Jobs Committee meetings.

Subsequent summer jobs campaigns were undertaken with Langendorf Bakery, Pepsi-Cola, Coca-Cola, a local linen supply company, and others. Each had its unique character, but the pattern was the same: seek a meeting; propose a number of jobs; negotiate; divide the number of jobs agreed upon in thirds of the summer; distribute the jobs using the point system. Failure to agree to meet, or failure to reach agreement would lead to direct action.

In the course of the summer, an MCO bread company boycott took products off the shelves of neighborhood grocery stores—and led driver-salesmen to complain to their employer that their commission income was being hurt. Pepsi manager Campodonico called the police tactical squad on us; we were escorted by them from the building. We shifted focus to San Francisco Mayor Alioto, demanded to know why the tactical squad was called on a legitimate community organization, and used his defensiveness to get agreement that he would call Campodonico and tell him he should meet with us. We added this touch; we want to be escorted by the tactical squad. The mayor laughed, but a cop showed up at the meeting. We had a negotiated power relationship; we respected each other.

Lesson: Go to the people who have what you want and propose that they provide it. Pick targets where your direct action can have an impact—hurting them in the pocketbook, the voting booth, etc. Position politicians so they have to decide whether or not they are on the people's side. We were already Alioto's negotiating partner on the Model Cities program. He didn't want our fight with Pepsi in the media where it would provide ammunition to moderates in his camp who opposed his deal with MCO.

Lesson: MCO direct action won important victories for the neighborhood merchant association (closing a main shopping street porno movie theatre and halting relocation of pawn shops from an adjacent urban renewal site); for tenants who were neighborhood church members; for block club members who wanted burned out or boarded up buildings torn down; for adult members of churches who got full-time jobs and more. MCO respected and won support from unions.

Mayor Alioto threatened to abandon the MCO-City partnership. He couldn't make the threat stick: moderates in MCO weren't willing to quit—as he requested of several of them.

INCOME

POVERTY POTLUCK: Battling Social Assistance Clawbacks in Canada
By Claire Gallagher

Like taking candy from a baby?

The British Columbia Liberals revealed their callous side when they did exactly that, with a policy change in 2002 that mandated child support clawbacks. Single parents receiving income and disability assistance were to have all of their child maintenance payments deducted from their income assistance payments, with harsh penalties for failure to disclose receipt of child support payments.

By 2013, more than half of the children in single-parent families in British Columbia were living in poverty. The child support clawback policy punished low-income single parents with disabilities and forced the Province's most vulnerable children into poverty. One parent estimated that $30,000 of child support payments had been diverted from their child over a ten-year period, as a direct result of the Liberals' cruel policy. By putting profits before people, the government ensured that university, extracurricular activities, and a better quality of life were out of reach for many low-income families.

The child support clawback issue was impacting BC ACORN members and in 2013 the organization mobilized to tackle this unfair policy. Members organized a series of monthly actions to apply pressure to the provincial government. They secured two meetings with the Minister of Social Development and Social Innovation, after five months of actions at social assistance offices and two coordinated phone blitzes where members flooded the Minister's office with calls requesting a meeting.

Allies were crucial to the success of the clawback campaign and BC ACORN coordinated efforts with First Call, the Elizabeth Fry Society, Raise the Rates, the New Democratic Party, the Community Legal Assistance Society, West Coast Legal Education Action Fund, and the Single Mothers' Alliance to build even more power. Actions taken by allies included filing a legal action in the BC Supreme Court, calling for the Union of BC Municipalities to endorse an end to the child support clawbacks, as well as rallies and meetings with decision-makers.

ACORN members tactically organized actions to highlight the cold-hearted nature of the government's clawback policy. Since many families were forced to turn to food banks—and cheap food lacking nutrition—as a result of government clawbacks, members hosted a Mother's Day Poverty Potluck. Food insecurity impacts one-third of female-led, lone parent families, increasing the likelihood of malnutrition and health issues such as diabetes and heart disease. The powerful event showcased the unhealthy foods that families were forced to feed their children, in a call for the policy to be scrapped.

Other actions included a nod to the Government's empty promise of putting families first, by leaving empty gift boxes outside a local Member of the Legislative Assembly's office. Four ACORN leaders made a trip to Victoria, BC, to have their story told in the legislature and to hear from Premier Christy Clark during Question Period. Child support clawbacks were put on the government's agenda as ACORN members also held a media session with Michelle Mungall, the New Democratic Party's Critic of Social Development. This event, and others, caught the media's attention. During the 18-month campaign, members generated approximately fifty stories in the press.

By June 2014, public interest in the campaign was heightening and ACORN members held a rally at the Liberal Party's' Disability Summit. After months of actions, thousands of emails and letters calling for the policy to be scrapped, media attention, and pressure from allies, the government caved, announcing that they would review the clawback policy.

Members were elated when, in the February 2015 provincial budget, the government pledged to end child support clawbacks for single-parent families receiving income and disability assistance, effective September 2015. After years of campaigning, ACORN members, supporters, and allies succeeded in returning approximately $13 million per year in child support payments to low-income families. Over 5,000 of the province's most vulnerable children benefited from this policy change.

Meanwhile, across the country in Ontario, Ottawa ACORN members have been organizing to end clawbacks there as well. Almost two million people in Ontario live in poverty, with one in four people with a disability affected. With the Ontario Disability Support Program (ODSP) offering a meagre $489 per month towards housing

or rent, many people with disabilities are forced into poverty. After a 2015 meeting with the Minister of Community and Social Services, ACORN members were convinced they would not win the housing allowance increase they had been fighting for, and members shifted their focus to call for increased employment income thresholds instead.

In Ontario, recipients of ODSP and Ontario Works (OW) are eligible to work for income. However, they are only allowed to keep the first $200 earned each month before the province claws back 50 percent of further earnings, a disincentive to work which traps low-income Ontarians in poverty. The clawback of hard-earned dollars from the pockets of Ontario's most vulnerable workers severely impacts recipients' ability to afford adequate housing and other basic necessities. In addition to an increase in income thresholds, members are also calling for increases to asset limits, to allow families receiving social or disability assistance to keep savings.

As in BC, members have mobilized to hold regular actions. With a strong message of "work is not a crime", members erected a mock jailhouse outside Ottawa's courthouse to symbolize the unfair punishment of low-income people trying to supplement their income. Members developed a social assistance committee to generate ideas for actions and to plan events that would highlight the need for change. A Poverty Picnic was held outside the disability office, where empty plates sat upon picnic blankets to emphasize the struggle of living in poverty: food can often be a luxury.

In 2017, the Ontario Liberal government announced increases to asset limits and income exemptions for cash gifts, allowing OW and ODSP recipients to keep some savings and accept support from friends or family members. The 2018 Liberal budget promised a 9 percent increase in social assistance over three years, an increase in income exemption by 150 percent, and full removal of asset limits for people with disabilities. Unfortunately, with the recent change in government and newly-elected Premier Ford yet to announce any plan for social assistance reform, the fight continues!

MINIMUM STANDARDS CAMPAIGNS
By Wade Rathke and Bill Pastreich

Perhaps the classic benchmark for an organization-building off-the-shelf campaign was the great minimum-standard benefit campaigns that some credit to Fred Ross, Cesar Chavez, and Delores Huerta of the United Farmworkers. These were for many years a staple in building the National Welfare Rights Organization (NWRO) into the largest membership organization of poor people in the United States during its brief history in the late 1960s and early 1970s.

The legal handle for welfare rights was the "equal protection" argument embedded in the US Constitution that essentially holds that where there is access to an entitlement that might have been discretionary in administration, everyone in the same circumstances should be able to receive the same benefit without discrimination. Simply put, if a social worker gave a welfare mother a check for school clothing in Brooklyn for her children in a state run and largely federally funded program, then a mother in Albany or Queens or Troy, New York, was similarly entitled. Same for furniture or household supplies or winter clothing or Easter clothing in Massachusetts if the welfare policies there allowed for such special needs payments.

What was good for any goose, was equally good for the gander.

After Citywide Welfare Rights in New York City won a number of these benefit campaigns on different issues, such victories established the minimum standards for what a mother on welfare should be able to receive for her family. Organizers codified the victories into forms that members could fill out and check off the items that they needed and should have received, but had not gotten. These minimum standards campaigns were invaluable in no small part because state and local welfare offices resisted applying the benefits widely therefore giving welfare rights organizations hugely successful and highly winnable campaigns.

Bill Pastreich, the founding organizer of Massachusetts Welfare Rights Organization, who preceded my brief stint as head organizer there, always argued that it was an organizer's job to "steal any good campaign whenever they could," and he absolutely grabbed the New York City effort and took it across Massachusetts to even greater success.

Which is not to say it was not a huge and difficult fight to win initially in Boston, because it was; nor that we always won. (The winter coats campaign was a significant defeat, painfully felt in Springfield in the fall of 1969 when I was organizing there). But once won, it could eventually be won everywhere if the campaign was engaged and pursued. It cost state welfare departments millions and ultimately triggered flat grant programs that eliminated special needs, and incidentally, eliminated this organizing tool used in building mass organization among welfare recipients in Massachusetts.

I reached out to Pastreich to get his analysis from his days at the Massachusetts Welfare Rights Organization, and as a former student and colleague of Fred Ross. Time and again he pulled similar campaigns together successfully along these lines in Boston and on Cape Cod in Massachusetts as well.

When asked to define the minimum standards or benefits campaign, based on what he put together for welfare recipients in Massachusetts, Pastreich said, "Minimum standards existed as an undefined right in the welfare department handbook. Theoretically it was there because the regular welfare grant was to cover food, rent, etc., but there was no way to use the grant to cover furniture, household supplies nor clothing."

The neighborhood-based organizing was straightforward. According to Pastreich, "The organizing in the neighborhoods focused on the right to special needs and building a list as to what the welfare department ever gave out in the past for furniture or household supplies. The list was developed by organizers asking if the welfare recipient they were visiting ever got anything. What was clear was that in order for the recipient to get anything, the recipient was required to show what they lacked first, and then submit three estimates of what it would cost for them to purchase the item."

Pastreich recalled, "The furniture forms contained a long list of items that organizers (all volunteers except myself) heard were ever given to recipients. The form was on 8½ x14 white paper with a large red "SAMPLE" printed diagonally across the page. Organizers would show the forms and talk about our plan to meet, elect temporary officers, fill out the official forms (blue), walk (march) down to the Welfare, demand a meeting for the temporary officers with the administrator, turn in the forms, and give them a week to check that the items are needed. We got prices for the furniture items from three downtown stores in Boston: Filenes, Jordan Marsh, and Gilchrists."

No surprise that the initial reaction of the welfare departments was less than positive. Pastreich described the tactics and strategies used in these campaigns to reach a successful conclusion.

"Our major tactic was to march on the welfare office for minimum standards, first, for furniture, followed by household supplies, winter and summer clothing, and so forth. Many of the marches around the state ended in sit-ins and arrests. We went en masse to the neighborhood welfare office," he recalled. The administrator would try to head people off in the lobby. We ended up talking to individual welfare workers and giving them the form and a week to check it. Having kept so close to the system (letting social workers visit to check the need, supplying three estimates, giving the social workers a week to check for the need) the reaction of the department was to give in (the fear of sit-in and riots certainly played a major role in Boston at that time)."

Unlike campaigns where tactics are used to get players to a negotiating table, the minimum standards campaigns, as described by Pastreich, didn't involve much in the way of talks.

"There were never really negotiations but rather fighting until the welfare office met our demands. For example, when we had over 250 recipients at our first sit-in at Roxbury Crossing in Boston, by 11:00 p.m. at night the Governor's African-American aide was there with us, the head of the welfare office was there, all the social workers (who were needed to give out vouchers for the items) were still there. The head of the state Welfare Department, Robert F. Ott, finally caved in and gave the social workers the order to give vouchers based on the three estimates. It became known as "Black Tuesday" at the state legislature and the "Day of the Bonanza" among Boston welfare recipients."

Over time, the procedures for minimum standards on welfare and even the prices became pretty well established in campaigns from city to city in Massachusetts.

As Pastreich recalled the process, "The system allowed the welfare workers—once verifying the need—to approve the vouchers. There was almost always one or more of them (known to us as the 'radical social workers') who would sit in with us, thereby giving us someone to approve the vouchers once the sit-in was won. Incidentally, the *Boston Globe* went out of their way to have photos of white demonstrators along with black ones. Those were interesting times."

The National Welfare Rights Organization (NWRO) also played a role in the city campaigns, making links among local allies and activists. Said Pastreich, "The NWRO served many purposes in the successes. Originally, it recruited me and paid my salary. George Wiley, NWRO director, introduced me to local activists and to a minister, Rev. Jim Breeden, who was helpful for both legitimacy and with money sources."

When asked to comment on the costs and the final outcome of the welfare campaigns throughout Massachusetts cities, Pastreich said, "I can't remember what the costs to Massachusetts were, although they were substantial. They were high enough that it provoked Governor Sargent to propose the flat grant, raising all payments in order to eliminate special needs that came in. The goal when I started the state organization (MWRO) was to develop minimum standards for the state to be used as an organizing tool. The state finally realized how well it worked and rolled the money it was spending on special grants statewide into the 'flat' grant."

Pastreich agreed that minimum standards campaigns could be adapted to other issues that involve entitlements or creating entitlements, saying, "There certainly are lots of potential issues one could develop as important rights that would be important enough for people to both fight to win and then to fight to keep. There are examples from my time later on Cape Cod that included government housing programs from both state and federal sources; medical care regardless of ability to pay (also known as the Hill-Burton Community Service Obligation). There were campaigns for the right to CETA jobs, and rights to mortgages, credit, and to eliminate liens by local hospitals, and other issues."

ACORN recently ran a similar minimum standards campaign in Rome, Italy, to win rent reductions for tenants, though landlords and courts have tried to rollback our victory in much the same way that welfare rights experienced almost fifty years ago [see David Tozzo's essay in this volume]. ACORN also attempted to develop other tenant-based minimum standard campaigns more recently in

Scotland to more moderate success. Mental health consumers with ACORN's MCAN affiliate pursued the same strategy in 2017 with the Alaska Mental Health Trust.

Scholars seem curiously divided on the value of minimum standard campaigns in building an organization, but not for any good reason that we can determine other than the need to put their noses in the air and substitute their biases for the enthusiasm of members for the benefits they could—and did—win. Regardless, understanding the nuts and bolts of minimum standard campaigns—how to build and engineer them should be part of every organizer's and organization's arsenal.

There is never a need to apologize or a reason to shy away from winning in undertaking campaigns to build organization and benefit membership.

FURNITURE FOR FAMILIES
By Steven Kest and Wade Rathke

ACORN's first big campaign was the Furniture for Families campaign in September 1970. In working with welfare recipients to build organizations, ACORN staff discovered that the state welfare regulations provided for a $40 annual emergency assistance allowance for each public assistance recipient. Could this $40 be used to buy furniture for families who needed it? ACORN members said yes. State Welfare Commissioner Len Blaylock and his legal advisors said no.

The ACORN groups in Little Rock and North Little Rock chartered city buses and descended *en masse* on the Pulaski County welfare office on a daily basis the first week of the campaign. Arriving one group at a time, they were determined to force Blaylock to agree with ACORN's demands. The welfare office was usually already overcrowded with lines of clients making applications and inquiries. The addition of over 600 angry ACORN members packed into the small building during the week swelled the office beyond capacity. The ACORN members passed out leaflets and their chosen spokespersons crowded into the county welfare director's office, made their demands regarding the $40 allowances and poured out other grievances as well, including bitter complaints of rudeness and unhelpfulness on the part of some welfare caseworkers. These demonstrations went on at intervals for several weeks. Blaylock and some of his aides came over and looked in on several of them.

In a larger action, the ACORN demonstrators then invaded the state welfare department's headquarters in the state capitol complex, crowding the halls, singing and passing out leaflets explaining the campaign and repeating the demands. They packed Blaylock's office, where he received them calmly. A few state troopers, mainly in plain clothes, constituted the only official acknowledgment of the potentially explosive nature of the demonstrations. The press was everywhere. On one occasion, the demonstrators moved over to the capitol where Governor Winthrop Rockefeller received some of the leaders.

Blaylock argued that the $40 emergency allowance could not be used for furniture and that even if it could be, there was not enough money to honor all such requests. He also objected to the methods, and accused ACORN's organizers of misleading the members about the regulations and the amount of money available. Nonetheless, ACORN was able to leverage the persistent actions into a meeting of ACORN leaders with the governor directly, where we did not get complete agreement but made progress.

Six weeks after the mass actions began, the campaign ended in a solid victory for ACORN. Rockefeller had come around to ACORN's position and clearly had decided either on the merits or on the politics that ACORN's demands should be met. Whether he did so because he believed in our cause or because he wanted to put an end to potentially violent demonstrations or because he was involved in a bitter re-election fight with Orval Faubus, is immaterial. The welfare department agreed that a need for furniture could be considered an emergency in some cases, and a new independent state agency was established by executive order of the governor, called Furniture for Families. It was charged with collecting used furniture from anyone who wanted to give it away or sell it for small sum; storing it and in some cases repairing it; distributing it free to any public assistance recipient who needed it, and delivering it for free.

ACORN had won its first major victory.

IT'S EXPENSIVE TO BE POOR: Fighting Predatory Lending
By Judy Duncan

When ACORN organizers door-knock, often the first and most frequent issues that come up are substandard housing, affordability, crime, and safety. However, after organizers spend a few minutes or hours talking about what people feel are the most important issues, deeper structural concerns sometimes arise like finances, banking, and how it's expensive to be poor.

Around 4.5 million Canadians are low-income. Up to 47 percent of Canadian workers live paycheck to paycheck. For many low-and moderate-income community members, this means they are one flat tire or unexpected expense away from spiraling debt. Often, lower income is linked to a lower credit score. In an emergency, how do you access money? If you have a good credit score, you likely have a line of credit (at steep interest) or maybe a credit card (at even higher interest), or overdraft protection (also at significant interest), but if you have bad or no credit, what are your options? Family and friends are options, but what if you don't have that option—what is next?

Robbie McCall's payday loan nightmare began ten years ago with a desire to buy his teenage daughter a special Christmas gift. Robbie had started receiving social assistance after health problems forced him to leave his job. A payday loan for a few hundred dollars seemed like a good idea. What wasn't made clear to Robbie was that interest on his loan was being calculated biweekly, so he was paying about 500 percent interest, not 20 percent as advertised. Two months later, he took out another payday loan, and dug himself an even deeper hole. This started the vicious cycle that so many Canadians with no or bad credit fall into. Soon Robbie was borrowing from one payday lender to pay back the other. It took Robbie three years to pay off $1,400. In the end he ended up paying more than $10,000 in interest.

Is this the payday loan business model? An Ernst and Young study for the Canadian Association of Community Financial Service Providers found that "the survival of payday loan operators depends on establishing and maintaining a substantial repeat customer base." The 2012 *Canadian Financial Capability Survey* revealed that 57 percent of payday loan users had taken two payday loans, while 20 percent had taken three or more loans.

In 2014, after the passing of her mother, Donna Borden ran into problems and needed a loan. She had growing debt because of supporting her ill mother. At the time, she had approached her bank to consolidate her loan payments to make it easier to repay. However, the bank told Donna that she had too much credit. Not *bad* credit, just too much. They wouldn't offer her a loan. Left with no alternative, Donna signed up for a $10,000 loan with CitiFinancial (now Fairstone). The interest rate was under the 60 percent permissible under the Canadian Criminal Code. Yet with the addition of thousands of dollars of insurance premiums, she soon realized it was going to be impossible to pay the loan back. She reached a point where she had repaid $25,000 for a $10,000 loan and CitiFinancial was saying she still owed the original $10,000. After searching every corner of the Internet to find out how she could resolve this issue, she found that there are few consumer protections in place to protect people from these unscrupulous lenders. She reached out to ACORN.

ACORN members like Robbie and Donna are just two of a large number of members who are not served by the mainstream financial system. Research shows that up to 15 percent of Canadians are "underbanked", meaning that while they may have access to a bank account, it does not meet their needs. The reasons for this financial exclusion include: high NSF (non-sufficent funds) fees ($48 at most banks); no overdraft protection for emergencies; geographic barriers; or no access to low-interest credit. As a result, many Canadians are financially marginalized and forced to rely on the services of alternative, high-interest lenders, as Robbie and Donna were forced to do.

Increasingly, low-income consumers are relying on forms of high-interest lending, such as payday loans, installment loans, car title loans, rent-to-own products, and others. Many of these alternative lenders operate in a consumer-protection gray area. Federally, the Canadian Criminal Code mandates that loans cannot exceed 60 percent interest. Payday loans are regulated provincially, with a maximum cost of $15 to $21 for every $100 borrowed, depending on the province. This equates to an annual percentage rate (APR) of 391 percent to 652 percent! There are an estimated 1,500 payday loan outlets across Canada, often clustered in low-income neighborhoods where banks are closing branches at an alarming rate. Payday loans are typically unsecured, small-value loans of up to $1,500 usually repaid by the next payday. They are the costliest form of lending in Ontario.

However, we are seeing a growth in new types of loans—likely because of increased regulation on payday loans. The financial reporting agency, TransUnion, has indicated that installment loan debt is growing faster than any other type of debt in Canada. In 2017, approximately 6.4 million Canadians had an installment loan. Installment loans are typically unsecured loans of up to $15,000, with set repayments over periods of up to three years. Interest rates can reach 59.9 percent, just below the legal cap. However, ACORN has encountered examples of additional fees and insurance costs taking interest rates beyond 60 percent.

ACORN's 2016 *Fair Banking Survey* of 270 ACORN members across Canada found that only four percent of respondents who use high-interest lending services prefer to use these services. The majority were forced to do so out of necessity. People indicated they turn to alternative lenders as a result of having no overdraft protection with their bank, no access to a credit card, or the more convenient location

of the alternative lender. The survey also found that 30 percent of respondents used high-interest alternative lenders, such as payday lenders to pay for food; 17 percent use them for housing; 16 percent for bills; and 10 percent as a result of poverty in general. Recent ACORN research has found that 25 percent of people who are experiencing crisis level debt—to the extent that they must seek professional assistance—have debt with a high-interest, alternative lender.

Thirty-seven percent of individuals experiencing crisis-debt have debt with Money Mart, the largest payday lender in Canada. Money Mart also offers installment loans. Thirty-two percent have debt with installment lender, Fairstone (previously CitiFinancial).

At a time where Canadians are racking up debt-to-income and are at a rate of 169.9 percent (an increase of over 93 percent since 1990), more and more low-income earners are being pushed into relying on fringe financial services that charge predatory rates.

Until now, the federal government's focus when regulating the banks has only served to push low-income communities further to the fringes. Changes to mortgage regulation look to make it even more difficult for low-income earners to access credit from mainstream financial institutions. The "mortgage rate stress test" was introduced to ensure that consumers can afford to borrow, yet by not moving forward on a regulatory framework that addresses the entire market—specifically the absence of a national anti-predatory lending strategy—the federal government has missed the mark.

The stress test only succeeds in raising the bar even higher for low-and moderate-income earners who strive to own a home. Even the banks admit it. Senior economist Robert Hogue, from the Royal Bank of Canada, stated publicly, "If you tighten rules and raise the bar on getting a mortgage from financial institutions, it may prompt a number of borrowers who are being shut out to deal with lenders that are in the less regulated space." In the midst of a housing crisis, this will push consumers further into the fringes and increase the risk that borrowers will get trapped in high-interest, high-risk mortgages. Analysts indicate that the entire fringe market is growing—with further growth expected over the next twelve months. ACORN members worry that without adequate protections in place, more people will be forced into the same predatory debt trap that Donna and Robbie were pushed into.

ACORN Canada's Fair Banking/End Predatory Lending Campaign calls for an inter-jurisdictional strategy to tackle the high-interest lending that further entrenches poverty within our communities. By taking coordinated steps, the municipal, provincial, and federal governments can work together to ensure access to fair financial services for low-and moderate-income Canadians.

At the municipal level, city councils can introduce regulations to limit the number of payday loan stores in the city, and restrict the number of licenses provided to payday lenders, as was done in Hamilton, Ontario. Municipal governments can also support the creation of alternative low-interest loan products.

The provincial governments must extend payday loan repayment, using a model similar to Alberta's repayment extension to sixty days. They can enforce the ban on rollover loans by creating a user real-time database to monitor and avoid rollovers from company to company. They can create protections for installment/rent-to-own/title loans and support the creation of alternative low-interest loan products.

The Canadian federal government must mandate the banks to provide access to low-interest credit for emergencies and low-interest overdraft protection. They must mandate the banks to provide no holds on checks; lower NSF fees from $45 to $10; and create alternatives to predatory lenders, such as postal banking and credit union credit products geared toward low-and moderate-income families.

In addition, the federal government must create a national anti-predatory lending strategy, create a real-time national tracking system (or database) to help stop roll-over loans, and amend the Criminal Code to lower the maximum allowable interest rate from 60 percent to 30 percent.

HEALTH: USING COMMUNITY ORGANIZING STRATEGIES TO FIGHT HOSPITAL DEBT IN WASHINGTON
By LeeAnn Hall

"Health care is the number-one cause of personal bankruptcy and is responsible for more collections than credit cards." – The Atlantic, 2014

The Affordable Care Act (ACA) gave organizers new handles for addressing hospital debt. The law introduced new requirements that nonprofit hospitals *must* meet in order to maintain their 501(c)(3) tax-exempt status. The IRS then adopted regulations implementing these provisions of the Act.

Some of the major requirements for nonprofit hospitals included: a written financial assistance policy that is well publicized; language access; an accessible application form and process; limits on hospital practices that create barriers to emergency care. The Act also placed prohibitions on nonprofit hospitals engaging in aggressive collections practices (except as a last resort) and required completion of a community health needs assessment to better understand the needs of the local community. The new federal rules did not specify eligibility levels or amounts of assistance to be provided, but they did provide new leverage for community organizations pursuing agreements to meet the needs of their low-income members.

> A couple of years ago, my husband had a stroke and I was diagnosed with cancer. We went to Swedish Hospital to receive the care that we needed. Thankfully, my cancer went into remission. However, I was left with thousands of dollars of medical debt. I tried to fill out a charity care application multiple times, but the process was long and confusing. The hospital wanted bank statements, copies of our bills, and other information that I didn't have readily available. I ran around trying to gather all the information to fill out the application, and when I sent it in, I never heard back as to whether I was approved or not. Now, Swedish-Providence calls constantly. I tell them that I cannot afford to pay, as every dime of our Social Security retirement goes to the mortgage, food, and utilities. This experience has left my family drained financially and emotionally. –Dixie Mitchell

Despite passage of the Affordable Care Act, and increased reimbursement for care through private insurance and Medicaid, hospitals continued to slap patients with exorbitant bills. After hearing dozens of stories like Dixie's, the members of Washington Community Action Network came together and organized to win groundbreaking policy changes with local hospitals. Certain hospitals in Washington simplified charity care applications, pulled patients' bills out of collections to forgive past debt if they qualified for charity care, hired financial counselors who specialize in charity care, and raised eligibility for financial assistance to up to 500 percent of the federal poverty level.

Beginning in 2013, the Washington Community Action Network took on the fight against hospital debt with renewed vigor. Washington CAN! heard repeatedly from members like Dixie who actually qualify within the hospitals' guidelines for assistance. Yet instead of getting assistance and help through charity care programs, their debt was handed over for collection and they faced harassment and lawsuits for debt. Often, the hospitals were in flagrant violation of state law. Washington CAN! began pushing hospitals to fulfill their charity care obligations and go beyond those minimal requirements so no Washingtonian has to suffer under the weight of hospital debt.

Washington CAN! launched its first campaign in Spokane, targeting two hospitals—part of the national Community Health Systems chain. Washington CAN! members and staff started by knocking on more than 400 doors in the city's lowest-income neighborhoods, which led to dozens of stories of medical debt and challenges accessing financial assistance. These outreach efforts surfaced three consistent themes: information about charity care wasn't accessible to patients, people who qualified for support were being given payment plans, and when they couldn't pay their debt was sent for collection. The outreach also surfaced a critical medical debt problem amongst homeless families.

Through a series of health care forums and community meetings, a local leadership team began to educate city council members, other public officials, and opinion leaders about the problem. At two community forums, Washington CAN! raised public discussion and shared stories. After community members held two public actions outside the hospital to visibly highlight the impact on patients, the CFO of the hospital agreed to meet with Washington CAN! members..

After two meetings, the community and hospital officials came to an agreement that the hospital would re-evaluate people whose debt had been sent to collections to assess their eligibility for charity care. If they qualified, the hospital would forgive or reduce the debt. The hospitals also agreed to shorten their charity care application to two pages, and post information in public places where it would be available to consumers. In addition, the hospital hired six staffers to help patients fill out applications for both charity care and health coverage.

Across the state in Tacoma, Washington CAN! uncovered outrageous stories including that of the Potter family.

> In 2010, my husband's health began to decline and within a short span of time we began visiting St. Joseph's regularly and despite having insurance through Medicare, we found our co-pays and deductibles hard to manage. Meanwhile, my husband Charlie's health struggles intensified and we discovered that the cause of Charlie's pain was pancreatic cancer. We were waiting to follow up with the doctor when the hospital told us in a letter that we have accumulated too high of a balance and that they would have to terminate his care at this point. I lost the love of my life.
>
> Unfortunately, Charlie's debt survived him. I received endless bills and calls from collectors for the debt Charlie acquired. The calls, the bills, and my feeling of loss were overwhelming. St. Joe's never offered charity care assistance; they offered us no help managing the debt that caused them to stop his care. I am still receiving calls from collectors for my husband's bills at St. Joseph's. –Toni Potter

Washington CAN! brought members like Toni together to challenge debt collections practices at two hospitals: Multicare, a hospital system already in hot water for putting liens on people's homes, and Saint Joseph's, a CHI-Franciscan hospital that was playing "hide the charity care program." Washington CAN! proceeded to put public pressure on the hospitals to do better. These activities included mass submissions of charity care applications, releasing a report billed in the press as "scathing" and comparing the hospital's aggressive collection practices to its very profitable balance sheet. Keeping the pressure on, they knocked on more than 1,000 doors, placed yard signs throughout the neighborhood and let the hospital know that more hard-hitting reports were on the way. Washington CAN! also helped build a community-labor coalition to push the hospitals to improve their community benefits.

Toni Potter was one of the members who re-submitted a charity care application as part of a group filing. After walking her application into the hospital along with faith leaders, elected officials, and other patients, she received a call from the hospital and nearly $50,000 in debt was forgiven. Responding to criticism and pressure, another hospital—a for-profit hospital—extended eligibility to patients at 500 percent of the poverty line and stopped the practice of overcharging uninsured patients. More demands around collections practices, interest charged to medical debt, point of service billing, and community oversight were advanced by the community.

Further north in Seattle, Washington CAN! members took on heavy-hitter Swedish, which had been purchased by Providence Health and Services—the third largest nonprofit hospital chain in the US. The current administration wanted to expand its beautiful hospital campus in the Central District, a historically low-income neighborhood, to build a high-cost specialty care and research center. The expansion raised questions about the nonprofit's commitment to community benefits, especially when low-income community residents still struggled with debt.

> Dixie lived down the block from Swedish. An eighty-year-old grandmother, she was about to lose her home because of her unpaid health care bills. Her husband had a stroke and she had cancer. And because of outstanding bills she limited treatments because she was afraid of the hospital and her growing debt.

After months of door-knocking, Washington CAN! community leaders kicked off a campaign putting up yard signs and engaging in creative actions designed to highlight the inherent inequities and leverage enough public pressure to negotiate for change. Members and staff produced a report reviewing the hospitals' charity care and community benefits and juxtaposing financial assistance practices with excessive CEO compensation. Community members set up a "debt carnival" with games passersby could play mocking the hoops that patients must jump through to get charity care. Next there was caroling of hospital president's neighbors with re-written classics and lyrics inspired by Dickens.

Building momentum, Washington CAN! leaders decided to get the word out to patients themselves and leafleted the lobby with the hospital's own charity care policy. The hospital reacted with a cease and desist letter threatening legal action. Undeterred, members reached out to elected officials on the Seattle City Council and in the state legislature, sharing their concerns about the environment and human impacts of the expansion plan. They got a handful of elected officials and additional allied organizations to respond, delivering a letter to the president and CEO renewing the demand for a meeting. After months of organizing, the hospital began meeting with Washington CAN! and neighbors to discuss ways to improve financial assistance and community benefits.

These campaigns are examples of what can be accomplished with community pressure, and the Affordable Care Act provided a renewed opportunity to fight back against hospital debt. The Act:

- **Provided a minimum set of standards.** Groups could put heat on hospitals to fill in the blanks set out by federal rules with strong affordable care/community benefits policies.
- **Included an enforcement mechanism that groups can leverage.** The new rules included possible loss of tax-exempt status or other penalties.
- **Required a community process.** The Community Health Needs Assessments hospitals were required to conduct include community involvement. Although hospitals have lots of latitude, this provided an opening for organizing and engagement.

Debt is not the only community need that can be met through such campaigns. Washington CAN! and its sister organizations have run campaigns that have addressed racial equity issues as well.

Those campaigns have included:

- Diversifying the workforce by having the hospital fund a scholarship fund for local Latino high school graduates interested in attending the local university and pursuing a career in

health care—with the goal of returning and working at the hospital.
- Negotiating an agreement that created culturally appropriate and family friendly accommodations for Native American patients and created space for indigenous religious practices.
- Improving translation and interpretation services—that include the charity care application process and extend into the medical setting to improve medical care for non-English speaking patients.

In evaluating these campaigns, leaders and organizers highlight these three key lessons:

- **Shedding a spotlight on stories is what moves a campaign.** At every opportunity, elevate the stories of those who have been affected and make it clear who is responsible for their struggles. Expose bad practices and break through the institution's public relations façade. Stories resonate with everyone, including: legislators who have power to introduce legislation affecting hospitals, donors to the hospital, all patients (even those who do not have any medical debt themselves). The stories are what moves people and therefore the campaign.

- **Persistence and creativity are necessary for building the public pressure and power to win.** Asking nicely one time for better billing practices won't work because the hospital will just assume they can brush you off easily or ignore you. Make it clear that you will not be ignored. In order to do this, plan on a series of escalating actions designed to highlight the experiences of patients, build public support and leverage the power of elected officials, the clergy, labor, and other community leaders. Consistent, creative actions keep the hospital administrators on their toes and push them into having a dialogue.

- **Our power is still in our numbers.** Strong, consistent public engagement of our members, allies, and elected officials that demonstrates strength in numbers creates the power to win.

THE AMBULANCE PLEDGE CARD SYSTEM
By Zach Polett

Health care is both a very good and a very difficult area for organizing. Very good, because it affects everyone (at one time or another), is the fastest growing part of the American low-to-moderate income family budget, and is a field rife with outrages and horror stories. Difficult, because it can be hard in the health care field to focus campaigns on issues that are specific and clear-cut enough to catch the imagination and understanding of the members sufficient to trigger their participation and the belief that they can win. Ambulance service is a specific, though certainly not all encompassing, aspect of the health café system that is well-suited for organizing. The ambulance service campaign conducted by ACORN in Fort Smith, Arkansas, in 1975, keyed around a Pledge Card System, might be of interest in looking for health care handles for campaigns.

The major issue, as reported by ACORN members who had to deal with the private ambulance company, was that they demanded money on the spot, and were very rude and insistent about it. There were some scattered cases reported of the ambulance company refusing to pick up people if they didn't have the cash, and some cases of precious minutes being wasted while the ambulance crew investigated where their money was going to come from. The majority of member complaints involved rudeness and intimidation of the victim, relatives, and friends once they got to the emergency room. Often the ambulance driver would refuse to leave the hospital room until paid. Drivers were told by the ambulance company management to tell people that they would not get paid for their night's work unless the victim's people paid them on the spot.

Thus, the goals of the campaign were first, to win a firm commitment from the ambulance company that there would not be even one second's delay with a sick patient over the question of the company's payment, and that harassment of the people at the hospital would have to end.

Secondly, we researched the ambulance company and its history to see who we were going to be dealing with and what possible targets and regulatory handles we might have. Our research revealed that we did not have the ideal target. It turned out that ambulance service in Fort Smith, a mid-sized Arkansas city on the western border of the state with Oklahoma, had been run for years by funeral homes, as a way to be first on the scene for new business (morbid, but true). This resulted in many problematic incidents, such as two funeral home ambulances fighting over who would get to take the perhaps soon-to-be-departed customer to the hospital. In the early 1960s the funeral homes started to drop out of the ambulance business and the city government, fearful that they would be left without an ambulance company, gave an exclusive charter with regulated rates to a local businessman, soon to be elected state Senator. He went broke, allegedly (and at least to some degree, actually) because he had such a high ratio of uncollected bills. A young fellow who had been a driver with the Senator's ambulance company then took over the franchise with a new ambulance company. He and his wife worked long hours at the company; he drove an ambulance himself, and though they were not on food stamps, neither were they rapidly on their way to being one of the richer tycoons in town. It became clear to us quite early that we did not have an ogre as a target or anyone with deep pockets, and that the guy probably really did want to provide a decent ambulance service for the town. If we didn't cut the campaign right, he would get more sympathy from the press and local officials than we would.

Therefore, we backed off from the "he's a pig" strategy that leaders had at one point been contemplating, and moved toward a "we've got a good constructive idea" approach with our horror stories as evidence that it was a good idea.

The idea was an ambulance pledge card system, through which ACORN members would be able to sign an ACORN ambulance pledge card committing to pay for any ambulance service used and the company would pledge not to ask for the money on the spot, but simply to send the family a bill.

The first action in the campaign was the set-up. An appointment was made with the owner of the ambulance company so that a half-dozen of the ACORN members could meet with him. The leadership for the action laid out our grievances, won a commitment that they "do not ask for money before getting the patient to the hospital" after some back and forth when a member told their personal horror story and the owner complained about nonpayment and his willingness to do anything that would increase his "paid-up percentage." We argued no harassment and billing by mail; he argued deadbeats and rising costs.

Following this exploratory action, we designed the details of the Pledge Card System. It would be similar in design and construction of an ACORN membership card with a stub part for the ambulance company to keep in its files, and a wallet-sized receipt card for the family to retain. It included a pledge by the family to pay the bill, and a pledge by the ambulance company not to demand money at the hospital, and required signatures by both parties. ACORN as an organization had no part in the agreement and in no way guaranteed anyone's bill, although in subsequent negotiations with the ambulance company, we did agree to "encourage" any of our people who used the ambulance service to pay the bill.

In the decisive action of the campaign, we invited the ambulance owner to come to the ACORN office for a meeting. When he arrived, he walked into a filled-to-capacity room with about thirty-five people there. We started with several individuals relating their individual horror stories, and then the main leader of the action presented the Pledge Card plan as a solution that would work to both his and our advantage. We had prepared a larger-than-life six-foot poster board blow-up of our sample ACORN ambulance pledge card which we presented to him and asked him to sign. We did not land a signature right there, since he gave the excuse that he would have to consult with his Board of Directors, but we did win a commitment that he would present it to them, and that he agreed it was a good idea.

We held the meeting at night, so that our people could attend. We didn't invite the press, but we had prepared one of the reporters so we had a story in the paper the next day announcing that the ambulance owner was in support of the ACORN Ambulance Pledge Card Plan. The article heaped praise on him, placing him in a box if he reneged on his private commitment, since it was now public. He was upset at the press, especially the television coverage of an ACORN leader upholding up a giant six-foot pledge card, explaining how the plan worked. He argued that it encouraged people not to pay their bills, but he couldn't publicly attack us because we had had only positive things to say about him and his company in public.

It took another month-and-a-half of negotiations over details—held out of the public eye—between ACORN leaders and the ambulance owner to finally win a full commitment to the try the plan, but the campaign was fundamentally won after the big action and press coverage.

An extra benefit of the campaign, in addition to winning an issue that most everyone felt was both important and right, was that the ambulance pledge card became an additional membership benefit for prospective dues-paying ACORN members and helped significantly in recruitment. Early in the campaign we had discussed the relative pros and cons of using the pledge care system as a membership benefit versus opening it up to everyone in the city. The ambulance company ended up making the decision for us by insisting that the pledge be restricted only to members of the organization on a trial basis. Thus, we were able to get some of the best of both worlds since it was only available to members, but we were able to describe it in the press as something that, once we proved it worked, could be extended to church groups and other organizations throughout the city. This good-citizen-motherhood-and-apple-pie image was useful to us at the time because it helped balance the scrappy, radical image that we were developing from some of utility rate campaigns and neighborhood fights with the city.

HOUSING: LANDLORD LICENSING IN CANADA
By John Anderson and Marva Burnett

For working people in Canada the housing crisis hits in two ways.

First, and most talked about, is affordability. In Canada's major cities like Vancouver, Ottawa, and Toronto, average home prices are over a million dollars. Rents rise fast as the city cores fully gentrify, as rent control laws are relaxed, and as the consequences of federal government's abandonment of social housing funding during the 90s ravages our communities.

The second is the quality of the housing. For the most part middle class people are spared this, so it does not get the attention that the affordability issue does. For low-to moderate-income people, housing conditions—landlords not fixing things, health hazards like mold and pests, elevators being busted, broken heating systems in the dead of winter—are things that cannot be taken for granted.

Early on in the development of ACORN Canada, the membership determined that they must fight for both *affordable and livable* housing in Toronto.

Fighting to improve municipal building code bylaw and enforcement systems was a highly successful organizing campaign for ACORN Canada. Not only did it improve living conditions for hundreds of thousands of tenants, but it allowed the once-fledgling organization to take hold in Canada's largest city, Toronto, and beyond.

Landlord licensing was something that had been done in jurisdictions in the USA, and the idea quickly caught on amongst ACORN's leadership. When we first started talking about a citywide campaign, ACORN Canada President Marva Burnett remembers thinking, "We have an opportunity here to create a system that deals with the substandard apartment unit problem systemically instead of fighting building by building; instead of going after the sprat let's go after the shark!"

Licensing landlords would allow the city to generate revenues—per unit fees of around $10 annually. That would pay for the added bylaw officers to do proactive inspections in the buildings. It also would create a penalty protocol for non-compliance. In Toronto those penalties now include escalating daily fines, and having the city do the repairs and charge the landlord on their tax bill.

The landlord licensing campaign also helped solve a fundamental problem with local tenant organizing. Tenants are transient for reasons both in and out of their control, and this makes organizing lasting neighborhood chapters, or building-based groups, very difficult over time.

A case in point is ACORN Canada's original drive in Weston. At its peak, ACORN had over eighty dues paying members in the two Weston high-rise buildings and won over $350,000 in rent abatements from their landlord. That was in 2005. Fast forward to 2018 and while many of the members involved with the campaign are leading the organization, nearly all had moved out and dispersed throughout the city. If Toronto ACORN was going to grow, it needed a citywide tenant campaign as its foundation.

Also, the prospect of having organized groups holding landlords accountable in Toronto's 3,500 or so buildings was never viable. In order for tenants to secure safe and healthy homes, the city had to become a partner with ACORN in protecting hundreds of thousands of high-rise residents in the city from landlord negligence.

In many cities, phase one of a livable housing campaign involves a focus on creating or improving bylaws that detail apartment standards for tenants. However, in Toronto, where the city already had comprehensive apartment standards, we ran phase two of a livable housing campaign focusing on enforcement. Licensing landlords and exacting a license fee in Toronto would allow the city to enforce already existing standards.

In cities like Ottawa, ACORN ran a successful phase one campaign to have the city expand its apartment standard bylaws to include kitchen appliances. The same situation repeated itself in Surrey, a working-moderate income community outside of Vancouver, where there were no apartment standard laws at all, triggering a British Columbia ACORN campaign that won basic building maintenance codes.

Since Toronto had comprehensive apartment standard laws, it allowed Toronto ACORN to focus on the enforcement of those laws. And over the course of the campaign, Toronto ACORN was able to use and create many replicable strategies and tactics.

The most effective was the establishment of the ACORN Political Action Committee (APAC) in 2006 in Toronto's ward eight. By tipping the electoral balance for a pro-tenant councilor over incumbents—a rare feat in Toronto politics—ACORN was able to send a clear signal that it was a political force in the city. This effort was the main force behind the city creating a policy for proactive inspections for apartments in the city. The benignly named Multi Residential Apartment Building Audits (MRAB Audits) fell short of being a bylaw and creating a dedicated source of revenue like a licensing system would. It did force landlords to spend millions doing repairs—no small feat—and laid the groundwork for more campaign success in the future.

In 2014 Toronto ACORN reinvigorated our canvass program and utilized it in a campaign in the lead-up to the 2014 municipal election. The canvass proved effective in obtaining tenant signatures and contact information, generating constituent phone calls to local city councilors, and boosting turnout to local events.

The 2014 Toronto municipal election did not go as intended, but indirectly lined up the campaign for success. The progressive candidate for mayor refused to endorse ACORN's Landlord Licensing Campaign. He did not share the strategic vision of targeting the controversial and polarizing incumbent mayor Rob Ford's base throughout the massive tenant community. In the end Rob Ford was diagnosed with terminal cancer, dropped out of the race, and was replaced by his brother Doug. Former Rogers telecom CEO John Tory won the race with ease. It did not look good for landlord licensing, when Tory refused to answer any questions on the subject.

At local board meetings, leaders insisted that the campaign must move forward and they started making an action plan. Marva Burnett recalls, "We didn't know if he was moveable but with thousands of apartments across the city in desperate need of repair it would take decades to deal with it on a case-by-case basis; the only solution was to get the people to move him!"

First up was to deliver to Mayor Tory the 2,500 tenant complaints our canvass team had collected, and to do so in his first full day in office. At the action, Marva Burnett barged through security guarding the front door of city hall, and got the complaints to Mayor Tory's office. It was all aired on Toronto's live TV news station CP 24. We won a meeting with the mayor's office, and the tone was set for the final push of the campaign.

Turns out that lead staff from the Municipal License and Standards (MLS)—who had been attempting to please ACORN since members first barged into their office in 2005—were starting to come around to the idea of a licensing system for landlords. The MRAB audit policy victories were slowly eroded under Ford. He cut the funding to a minimum and MLS staff and officers did not have the tools to enforce the property standards. Exactly!

Throughout 2015 Toronto ACORN meticulously made lists of councilors who were for, against, or on the fence of the campaign. We then solidified the progressive votes on council once and for all. We knew we had a few conservative "haters" who we would not be able to move, so we forgot about them. The mayor's office told us in no uncertain terms that he would not be supporting the campaign. But, as he would learn throughout his first term in office, the Mayor of Toronto is just one vote on council. We set our sights clearly on the large bloc of centrists on council. If we won them over, we would win the campaign.

Organizers and leaders went to work in targeted wards, starting with councilors who were members of the Licensing Committee, which was the first major hurdle. The strategy was to highlight problems that exist in buildings in the targeted wards, and force the councilors to choose a side; either support families having healthy and safe housing or support slum housing conditions and their greedy landlords. This is where the long history of ACORN in these buildings came through and the media ate it up. Councilors knew that even the homeowners in their ward looked at the conditions in the apartment buildings in horror.

A pivotal moment in the campaign was when we unveiled the bipartisan team of "councilor champions" at a press conference held right before a key License Committee meeting. One by one they came up and pledged allegiance to the ACORN members dressed in their red shirts who were gathered outside of the committee room. First up was Josh Matlow, a Liberal who had a good relationship with our allies at the Federation of Metro Tenants' Association. Second was long-time NDP ally on council, Janet Davis, who had some infamous slumlords in her East York ward. Last up was Frances Nunziata, the Rob Ford-backing councilor in Weston who had known ACORN longer than any other politician in Canada. ACORN succeeded in making the issue not about left versus right, but about right versus wrong, which is critical when your allies don't control council and you've got to win a campaign.

The Licensing Committee passed a motion calling on staff to finalize a licensing bylaw that would be voted on at the upcoming City Council meeting.

After the success at the committee level, it was clear we had the broad support we needed, so ACORN members went to work having meetings with all councilors in the city. The breadth of the organization was on display, with local tenants meeting with their councilors to explain the problems in their buildings, talk up the merits of licensing, and asking their councilors to sign our pledge. If we didn't have leaders in a ward, we'd door knock and quickly find some tenants willing to help, and to join the organization.

As the meetings went on, and pledge after pledge was signed, it became clear that we had the votes to win at council.

In order to drive home our point, Toronto ACORN released a report called *State of Repair*, which summarized results of an online tenant survey we did through our ever-expanding email list. The results on the front page of the *Toronto Star* really drove our campaign home. Forty-five percent of tenants see cockroaches in their units at least once a week; 53 percent have heating problems in the winter. And the real doozy, 28 percent felt too threatened by their landlords to even file a complaint, driving home the need for proactive municipal enforcement. We were making it increasingly difficult even for the closest landlord-aligned councilor to oppose us.

ACORN started having tenant "speak-outs" in buildings across the city. When kids were coming home from school with parents, our leaders would set up tables in their building lobbies, draped with an ACORN flag and filled with information on the campaign. And we'd start generating phone calls to targets. Tenants would call in a complaint to city bylaw enforcement offices and to their landlord directly, as well as call their city councilor asking them to support the campaign. The members would also have tenants check off, on a larger poster board taped to the wall, the repair issues they had in the building. If a landlord did show up to the "speak-outs" our members would start chanting and deliver a demand letter asking for a list of repairs to be done. The "speak-outs" were even simpler than a classic ACORN quick hit and allowed the membership to get deeply involved in the campaign. The councilors took notice.

The day of the final council vote, our math showed we had a wide majority of councilors on our side. Our members went to city hall in their red shirts to watch the vote. After waiting through some mundane agenda items, it was our time. In the end only three councilors voted against us, and thirty-seven were in favor. The mayor made a deal with our allies that he would also vote in favor as long as they did not publicly embarrass him about the loss. Just prior to the vote councilors took turns congratulating the ACORN members in attendance. A motion was passed to have tenant engagement money set aside for tenant organizations, as well as a motion accepting a suggested name for the new enforcement system, namely, RentSafe T.O.

The struggle never ends, and licensing landlords isn't solving all of Toronto tenant problems, but it has put millions upon millions of private landlord dollars into making our members' homes livable. The campaign also built Toronto ACORN into a permanent and powerful force.

FIGHTING FOR RENT CONTROL IN SANTA ROSA
By Davin Cardenas

While the North Bay Organizing Project leaders were doing voter engagement in our neighborhoods, we came across an apartment complex of eight families who were having their rent increased by $500, while dealing with roaches, rats, and black mold.

The tenants started meeting on a regular basis to figure out what to do. They declared, "No Rent for Rats!" and went on a rent strike for two months to launch their campaign. We talked about our struggle in churches, *quinceñeras*, and the vineyards where tenants work. Other apartment complexes came forward with complaints about evictions and joined the fight. We continued to act. We took direct action on the landlord and marched to the City Hall.

In 2016 the tenants successfully forced the Santa Rosa, California, City Council to take a stand and pass a rent control policy that the tenants themselves had helped develop. In 2017 the original tenants won a $2.75 million lawsuit against the landlord. Now we're creating a countywide Santa Rosa Tenant Association to fight for rent control for all renters.

Here is what we learned in the process of the campaign.

Little flames build a fire

Our campaign was founded in a complex of eight units, eight families who decided to organize, rebel, and make their rebellion public. They were clear at each step of the way—their rent strike, their direct action on the landlord, their march to the city hall—that they were not only acting on their own behalf, but also so that others would do the same. The public aspect of their actions, and the actions of many tenants to come, would begin to shift public consciousness and bring the crisis to the top of the city's priorities. After this first flame, we were able to highlight more stories from others in Santa Rosa, in Healdsburg, in Petaluma—all in very public ways.

Diversity is our best defense

As with any healthy natural ecosystem, diversity allows for healthy roots systems and flourishing ecology. So too, in our struggle, did the diversity of our forces demonstrate a cross section of mutual self-interests. Stories told at rallies, in "Close to Home" articles, on radio and TV, all varied from displaced farm workers, to sympathetic landlords, to indignant clergy, to homeless church members, to senior citizens being crunched on Section 8 housing. This diversity also reflected the love for the diversity of our city, and a dignified stand against its transformation into a playground for the rich.

Culture precedes policy

A cultural shift—a shift in the ways people think, act, and talk—is usually the necessary predecessor to large-scale policy change. Through the use of theater, art exhibits, marches, news articles, public meetings, music, and small tenant victories, we were able to shift the way renters were talked about and how our grassroots leaders thought about themselves. We shifted how public officials began engaging around the issue, how hesitant allies came around to supporting the issue. Culture, like power, is a neutral element to be molded, and in the case of our current society, reclaimed and recaptured the needs of the people.

Those who buy ink by the barrel, also drink whiskey by the handle

Though dominant media is often an instrument of business interests, it can also be populated by journalists of integrity—people who haven't been completely marginalized by cynicism (or may want to counter their cynicism with a hard-hitting piece every now and again). These same journalists of integrity often also share and populate the same watering-holes as we might—they might even share common hobbies, even political sympathies. We must be willing to engage, build relationships, buy them drinks when possible.

Public officials have feelings too

Public officials are as affected by the personalizing of issues as any of us might be. We must be willing to engage to both polarize and depolarize, and develop sincere allies within the political class, while publicly holding accountable those whose interests hurt the working and middle class. Both of these should always be dignified and strategic acts, activities engaged in by people who care about transformational power and are able to distinguish between public and private relationships. We are not petty protesters, we want real power to be able to shape our own realities based on our values. The most privileged classes are always the first to ask that we avoid divisiveness, that we act nice, as though the current economy of evictions, low wages, ecological extraction, and war was not divisive in itself.

Voting as a bargaining chip

De Tocqueville said that voting was the weakest link in the democracy, essentially meaning that democracy required much more than the simple act of voting every couple of years. However, our organizations ability to engage in broad and targeted voter engagement was actually key in giving us greater voice, greater leverage, to be taken seriously at all levels of the local political scene. Our strategic focus on the most marginalized precincts through canvassing, community events, newspaper distribution, and follow up phone calls served as an alert to the local political class that we planned on shifting voting habits and the way local democracy worked. This played into the self-interest of local council members who were, or would become, pro-rent control public officials as well.

Soon after the council passed the rent control policy, the California Apartment Association paid fraudulent and devious signature gatherers to block the policy, and force a special June election in 2017. We lost by 781 votes, with historically low voter turnout numbers.

The struggle continues. We hope to see rent stabilization and "just cause" eviction policies put before the voters in a very near future, especially since our city suffered a devastating wildfire in October 2017 that wiped out five percent of the housing stock causing rents to skyrocket up 40 percent immediately.

.

ORGANIZING FOR WATER RIGHTS IN THE PARIS SUBURBS
By Adrien Roux

Twelve million euros per year will be paid by transnational water management corporation Veolia to the 200,000 low-income families living in North Paris suburbs. That's what we won after months of mobilization by the Alliance Citoyenne, ACORN France, its members, and allies.

In 2016, the inhabitants of Aubervilliers launched their long battle over water management in the Seine-Saint-Denis district. In mid-June 2016, each of the 30,000 tenants of Aubervilliers social housing received an invoice—a reconciliation of charges for water usage covering the period from 2012 to 2015. During these years no annual reconciliation had been made between billing estimates and actual usage. Now, suddenly, the tenants were facing huge bills. For some of them, the total amounted to over €1,500! Many panicked. "We cannot pay such large sums. We are tenants of public housing. Why this much? This is a management error by the housing corporation—it's not fair that it falls on us like this!"

The first neighborhood meeting took place in June after our organizing drive. And the eighty participants decided to make this water bill issue their top priority.

A large number of tenants had already visited the housing office to ask for explanations and make claims. They felt they had not been heard, and the uncertainty associated with these invoices remained unresolved. At the big meeting the organization decided to take on this issue: we would go together the housing office, demand explanations, and require that tenants' questions and difficulties be taken into account.

At the first action the manager invited tenants to enter the meeting room. They deposited bottles of water on the table, saying, "Your water is too

expensive, we prefer to return it to you." The manager accepted some of the group's demands and proposed a compromise on others. First, the amount of the invoices was reduced by about half when he agreed to cancel the reconciliation for the years 2012 and 2013. Then it was agreed that payment of invoices would start only at the end of October, the time when the office checks applications from all tenants appealing bills. It was also agreed that payments could be in monthly installments of €20 for everyone.

But after this initial victory, a question remained: Why is the water costing so much?

After investigation, we realized a cubic meter of water cost €4.26 in the suburbs while in Paris it cost only €3.41. Yet the median income of our Parisian neighbors is much higher than that of Albervillariens. Why? Because Paris has a public management system while the management of the Saint Denis district water system is contracted out to the transnational, French-based corporation Veolia.

Early in 2017, the battle for water started again and changed in scale and focus. Two hundred residents of Aubervilliers neighborhoods repeatedly held actions against their elected officials and the town hall expressing concerns over the high-water prices and the issue of contracting out to Veolia. They called and visited literally every local MP and regional, district, and city elected officials, offering them some bottles of precious water, and asking them their position on the water management system. During the April/May general elections, the eight local MP candidates saw it as a compulsory stop to respond to our invitation to come to an Aubervilliers neighborhood assembly to defend their position on the water management system.

None of them were decision-makers on the matter, but they were keen to agree with the inhabitants and stand with them for their right to the water. That helped increase support for the campaign and the people's demands. The matter became the top issue on the local political agenda during the summer. The mayor finally agreed to hold a public debate on the issue in September, and then the entire municipal team stood against the renewal of the contract to Veolia.

This switch in position by the second largest delegation of elected officials to St. Denis Plaine Commune district (which includes eleven cities) was a tremendous breakthrough and obliged other progressive elected officials to change their position on the matter. Public pressure carried on with continuing actions by the residents of Aubervilliers. These actions were coupled to the ongoing work of the coalition, "Public Water for Saint-Denis," and activities of a regional Water Coordination that targeted the other elected officials in St Denis district. On December 19, 2017, the majority of left-wing municipalities in the district voted to suspend their membership in the regional water association (Sedif), which subcontracts to Veolia, and announced plans to return to a public system of water management.

This victory was a landmark that put the small Alliance Citoyenne community organization among the public actors in Paris' northern suburbs.

Citizen actions such as these have multiplied since the creation of the alliance. In Paris' northern suburbs as in other French cities and in the world, is the old ACORN motto, "the people shall rule."

PROPOSITION H: Building Tenant Power in San Francisco
By Randy Shaw

San Francisco has such strong tenant protections that many do not realize the struggles it took to secure them. Prior to 1992, the city's roughly 70 percent renter population lacked the electoral base to win pro-tenant ballot initiatives. Since 1992, nearly every measure to strengthen rent control and eviction protections has been passed by voters.

What changed? 1992 saw the emergence of a newly structured tenants' movement with new strategies for success. And that has made all the difference.

Background

Prior to 1992, San Francisco's tenant activists were so convinced that the big money raised by landlords would defeat renter measures that they avoided the ballot and instead focused on passing legislation at the Board of Supervisors. This strategic analysis dominated the effort to enact rent control on vacant apartments (vacancy control), the central dividing line for San Francisco politics in the 1980's.

The limits of this approach became clear when Mayor Dianne Feinstein twice vetoed vacancy control without activists then going to the ballot. When vacancy control finally reached the ballot in 1991, it was put there by a referendum that landlords succeeded in qualifying for the ballot after the Board of Supervisors passed vacancy control in 1991.

Allowing vacancy control to go to the ballot in a non-presidential election year made no sense, as local election turnout is skewed to older homeowners and more conservative voters. But that's what the city's tenant movement did. Not surprisingly, vacancy control lost by a landslide in November 1991.

In response to this defeat, I joined others who worked full time for tenant organizations and began rebuilding the city's tenant movement. We made three key changes.

First, we vested power of decision-making in the city's housing counseling groups rather than in activists who often lacked a grassroots base. The latter model had empowered individual representatives of large apartment buildings despite their lack of capacity to mobilize others or to run winning campaigns.

Second, we realized that winning tenant ballot measures required expanding our base beyond core tenant neighborhoods. While this seems obvious, prior losing tenant campaigns targeted neighborhoods where campaign volunteers lived, which were heavily tenant neighborhoods. I moved to San Francisco during a 1979 rent control campaign and was told to drop literature in my home precinct bordering the Mission. But the "walk your precinct" strategy meant that swing voters in high turnout areas—the ones who decide elections—were not prioritized.

Third, we felt that the established citywide tenant political groups had become disconnected from the base. To remedy this, we held neighborhood tenant "conventions" across the city to find out what people wanted on the ballot. The process resulted in a ballot measure that responded to the city's high rents by cutting in half the guaranteed annual rent increase awarded to landlords under the city's rent law.

The problem was that while annual rent hikes were set at 60 percent of the Consumer Price Index, landlords got a minimum 4 percent annually regardless of inflation. Our measure eliminated the 4 percent floor. Our neighborhood conventions found that tenants were unaware that they had been paying rent hikes for the past decade that were double the inflation rate. Their knowledge soon turned to outrage, and a commitment to pass a ballot measure to stop this injustice—Proposition H.

Talk beyond your base

We saw "Prop H's" road to victory as running through the moderate Richmond neighborhood of San Francisco. No prior tenant ballot measure had prioritized the Richmond, which was a heavily Asian-American district where few tenant activists lived. Our early campaign poll found Richmond voters split on Prop H, so we made it our top priority. Our campaign mantra became "as the Richmond goes so goes the election," and it proved true.

Targeting the Richmond meant driving volunteers far from where they lived. It meant messaging targeted to homeowners and more affluent renters. Overall, it meant our campaign was talking beyond our core base. This was something prior tenant ballot measures had failed to do, but it is how over a dozen winning campaigns have proceeded since 1992.

Why do so many progressive campaigns not primarily target the swing voters that decide elections? In my experience many activists are so focused on not ignoring their base or taking the base for granted that they misallocate campaign resources. In actual elections the core pro-tenant vote had been pretty constant, yet this insecurity about the base shifted campaigns away from where outreach was most needed.

Think big

In addition to the specific strategies that built a winning initiative campaign, "Prop H" highlights the importance of thinking big. The right-wing understands this well. It puts sweeping measures on the ballot to defund public employee unions, eliminate affirmative action, and completely alter every aspect of state government with property tax restrictions (like California's Prop 13).

Progressives put far fewer big picture measures on local and state ballots. And when we do—as with the many minimum wage hike measures—we often win. Why are there not more progressive initiatives? I think the mentality that San Francisco tenant advocates had in the 1980's—"we can't win a ballot measure due to big money opposition"—is widespread. "Prop H" ended up being outspent $300,000 to $30,000 but it won. Rarely has the power of grassroots activism to overcome big money been better demonstrated.

It's always popular to put money in people's pockets, and that's what our "Prop H" did. Nearly all annual rent hikes since 1993 have been under 2 percent, and "Prop H" has caused the greatest shift in wealth from landlords to tenants in United States history.

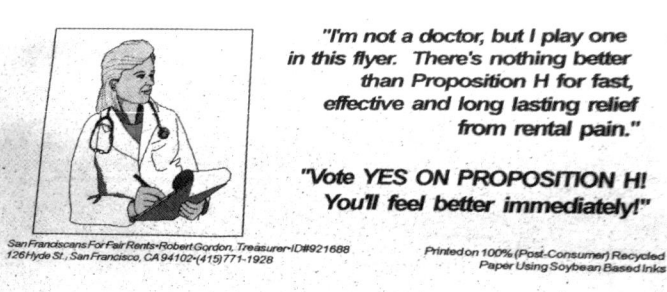

The populism of rent control campaigns

After studying virtually every California ballot measure through the 1990's, I realized that nearly all winning campaigns had one fact in common: they appealed to the self-interest of a significant portion of the electorate. Rent control and just cause eviction campaigns fit this thesis perfectly. Both directly benefit a city's renters, a substantial percentage of which have a self-interest in voting for such measures.

This helps explain why rent control campaigns are now sweeping California cities. All require support from homeowners and affluent renters to win. San Francisco's Prop H campaign created a template for tenant victories that is replicable elsewhere. California's November 2018 ballot includes an initiative (Proposition 10) to repeal the 1995 Contra-Hawkins Act, which prohibits cities from imposing rent control on vacant apartments. Backers of "Prop 10" are thinking big, talking beyond their base, and are using the grassroots strategies that brought victory on "Prop H".

ACORN HOME SAVERS CAMPAIGN: Old Wine in New Bottles?
By Dine' Butler and Wade Rathke

ACORN International launched the Home Savers Campaign—a housing justice campaign in the United States—in the spring of 2017. The campaign unfurled from conversations among ex-ACORN leaders and ex-Contract Buyer League organizers from the late 60s and early 70s, when the term land contracts began popping up more and more throughout the Midwest and the South.

Fifty years previously, before the passage of the Community Reinvestment Act, redlining was still national public policy administered by the Federal Housing Authority (FHA), and contracts-for-deed and similar contracts were predatory, pure and simple. ACORN wanted to see if the latest versions were the same or different. A volunteer army was formed to research potential victims of predatory contracts and hit the doors in various places around the country to ask folks what they knew about their housing agreements.

The idea of the campaign started with a few simple goals: to hear from people in these predatory contracts; to find out what they understood about the contract terms; to review their signed agreements and determine what the actual terms were; and to find out what the contract holders wanted to do moving forward. First, we targeted the two largest national companies: Vision Property Management (VPM) and Harbour Portfolio in cities where the campaign had institu-

tional relationships with community-based organizations or potential local allies. These cities were Philadelphia, Pittsburgh, Cleveland, Cincinnati, Youngtown, Atlanta, Detroit, Memphis, and Little Rock.

From the original doorknocking blitzes, we found that people, for the most part, did not understand what they signed. Many thought —and were promised—that they would own their houses upon the last payment of their current contract. This was not true under many of the contracts, especially those that were lease-purchase options. After reviewing several agreements in different cities, we found that they would not own their home at the end of the lease period, but instead would owe a balloon payment of several thousand dollars and need to either refinance or walk away.

We targeted VPM because most of the contracts would expire sooner so we had less time to try and save the homes. VPM contracts are generally seven years, whereas Harbour Portfolio contracts were thirty years. In order to prevent more people from losing their homes, the organizing strategy evolved building organizing committees of VPM contract holders in each city.

The ACORN Home Savers Campaign worked with people to better understand their contracts and asked them how they wanted to change their precarious homeownership status. Most expressed the desire to change their contracts so that one day they would become homeowners, build equity in their homes, and have their payments recorded with the credit bureau.

Each contract holder signed on to a letter to Vision's management demanding a meeting in their individual cities to renegotiate their contracts. At the same time, we put pressure on Fannie Mae to bar any company from participating in future auctions of foreclosed properties that intended to use "as is" installment land contracts to dispose of the inventory they might have acquired. When Fannie Mae agreed to reject such companies, that action cut off Vision's supply of additional houses. The company also came under a lot of pressure due to a *New York Times* series that exposed these contracts and other issues with the company's business model in Baltimore.

The confluence of these events meant that within weeks our demand letters were met with a request to meet in person. Our top committee members and our lead organizers headed to Columbia, South Carolina, to meet with Vision and to demand change. After several sessions, ironically, we found that we had some common ground between the campaign and company: both of us wanted to get contract signers out of the current agreements into some form of mortgage. We wanted our members to have title to their homes and be out from under the terms of a predatory agreement, and the company needed their contract holders to convert to mortgages as well so that it could access cash to pay off its investor pools.

The surprising recognition by both parties did not solve all the problems magically, but did lead to an agreement to modify the contracts so they were more transparent and fairer. Steps were taken to use lease payments to establish credits. Several pilot programs were negotiated. The pilot programs were focused in Michigan and Ohio to accelerate the process of conversation to ownership, with ACORN and Vision playing equal roles. Members overwhelmingly endorsed the agreement, and we continue to work with the company to change its basic business model in such a way that it facilitates a path of rehabilitation of properties in depressed neighborhoods and offers a quick pathway to affordable terms and ownership for families.

The lesson we learned by conducting this campaign was that sometimes the organizing stars align and you have to be organized and ready with committed leadership ready to pounce on corporate targets with a realistic set of demands that target a set of winnable organizational goals. You have to be open to the idea that companies and their leadership may actually want to change their practices—or can be forced to change.

Additionally, the organization must come up with a program and a plan to keep both sides accountable to the contract.

We met with Vision on the one-year anniversary of our signed contract and realized that our teamwork has successfully helped ten Vision contract holders succeed in obtaining mortgages, whereas before our project the likelihood of these families owning their homes was infinitesimal. Vision has doubled down on their commitment to building affordable housing for working families, and we will work with them on building an affordable housing program in Detroit, Michigan, and in northeast Ohio as well, by "rehabbing" land bank and abandoned properties and qualifying families to own them long term. At the same time, we continue to visit contract holders and work them through the conversion process from the lease-purchase options to actual mortgages putting the titles in their hands now.

There is no love in the relationship, but there is a grudging respect and increasing understanding—and acceptance—of the priorities on both sides of the table. The campaign is different than fifty years ago, but this time besides dealing with more stable housing and ownership for individual families, we are trying to see if we can forge a new model to once again put "people who need houses into houses that need people."

TENANTS CASH IN BY BREAKING THE BLACK MARKET IN ROME
By David Tozzo

Italy might well be one of the best countries on the planet for living.

And it might as well be one of the worst countries in the world for housing.

For decades now, there has been no way, no law, to counteract the illegal black market for renters, and the market turned itself into a disaster of big proportions and bad intentions which is the biggest and worst slice of the bitter cake that is tax evasion in Italy to this day.

Italians are heavy homeowners; 80 percent of the population owns at least a small apartment, and investing in "the brick" has historically been perceived and pursued as the most desirable and reliable form of investment for family or personal savings (another particularly Italian phenomenon).

What do the Italians do with their houses? Of course, they typically rent them out to generate income. Since the global economic crisis, such income has become increasingly crucial in providing a living, often—given extensive job losses—remaining as the last source of sustenance for many Italians for the time being.

Has the crisis worsened yet another Italian phenomenon, the illegal "black rents" market—renting out an apartment without paying the taxes due on it?

Actually no, it hasn't; the hateful habit has been standing shameless and strong for what seems like forever—a never-ending nightmare living outside of logic, legality, and reality.

The research institution CGIA of Mestre estimates the number of apartments, houses, and holes-of-any-kind rented out illegally nowadays at around a million. These houses are virtually empty as far as the Government knows, though it shouldn't be so easy to hide a house, and well, it really isn't, but at the same time it is.

Call it creativity. Or fashion. Or shame.

Fast forward to June 7, 2011, when one of former Prime Minister Berlusconi's ministers introduced the third article of a new law containing the unprecedented attempt to fight back against the black market for rental units. At long last tenants could report their black rent to the fiscal authority, Agenzia delle Entrate, and by declaring themselves illegal tenants could pay a fine for their own small non-payment. They would receive unilaterally (obviously without landlord consent or signature) a brand new and finally legal tenancy agreement of 4+4 years (a standard four-year lease with an automatic four-year renewal option), at roughly a fifth of the price of what they used to pay illegally. Yes, that meant tenants who paid up until that moment say, 1,000 euros, would start paying barely 200 euros or so for eight years to come.

Unprecedented. Unexpected.

Immediately, I knew we had a campaign to introduce community organizing in Italy. To cut a long story short, I got in touch with the folks at ACORN International and ACORN Italy was founded on September 12, 2011.

Not the typical community organization effort, the nationwide campaign to inform people of this hidden pearl of a law and to encourage tenants to become our members and register their contracts was terrific, skyrocketing us in the press and bringing in more and more members each passing day.

Then the backlash began and we woke up to a nightmare on March 10, 2014, when the Supreme Constitutional Court of Italy ruled the law unconstitutional, based on technicalities. The supreme justices, while maintaining that the law is no less than revolutionary in fighting the illegal rent market, found a glitch in how the law was written by Berlusconi's comrades, and they struck it down.

The immediate consequences were literally tragic: thousands and thousands of tenants (and ACORN members) were suddenly holding null and void leases. They risk being evicted in record time—in some cases from houses they have lived in for a lifetime. And, last but not least, they might well have been forced to give back all the amounts they saved each month. Let's say with your new tenancy agreement you were saving 800 euros per each month? Recall the law was in effect beginning three years earlier? The math—and money—was devastating for tenants to contemplate.

ACORN Italy immediately acted. A sit-in at the Ministry of Economy and Finance obtained the immediate result when our delegation was received by the Sottosegretario or Under-Secretary Enrico Zanetti. We were assured that the Government wouldn't allow any damage to thousands of citizens who in good faith, courage, and civic responsibility had reported their illegal rents and landlords to the state authorities.

In record time, barely two months after the Supreme Court struck down the law, the parliament passed a safeguard law which would save the contracts and their effects until December 31, 2015.

Fast forward again to late June 2015: the judges ruled one more time, and they also deemed the new safeguard law unconstitutional. Again, of course, on a technicality.

The Armageddon was back, but ACORN does not back down. We immediately took action again.

In reality even if it seems normal for Italians to evade each and every tax on rents (despite the fact that rents are the main source of income for the nation), we can't see the country returning back to black market rents, especially after the first law, albeit technically flawed, has been initiated to thwart this unbeatable cancer. This can't become the status quo again or return as our new reality. It can't be the standard.

The United Nations has determined that housing is a human right. A civil right can't be made illegal. For this reason, we have begun working towards reintroducing a law that our community of tenants and decent citizens deserves.

The Supreme Court of Italy referred to the law as revolutionary. Revolutions can't be allowed to fall or fail for technicalities.

Postscript
The fight has continued.

At the end of that year 2015, we made a last-ditch effort to again update the national law on this matter and introduce the issue into the annual national budget, which became law and took effect as of January 1, 2016. The "safeguard" law we had written acknowledged that each tenant did have to pay an amount for the time she stayed in the vulture landlords' homes, but that amount... had already been paid, corresponding to the relatively small amount the original law had already decided was owed.

Finally, on April 13, 2017, for a third time the Supreme (Constitutional) Court of Italy ruled on the matter, and this time, for the first and definite one, they ruled decisively in our favor.

Not an extra cent was owed by our members and tenants across the country.

Not the final battle of the war on dishonest landlords, but a hard fought one, and a decisive victory for ACORN Italy and Italy itself.

RIGHTS AND SAFETY CAMPAIGNS FOR WOMEN, YOUTH, AND IMMIGRANTS

RAPE, RESISTANCE, AND ORGANIZING
By Beth Butler with Ruth Rinehart

The #MeToo movement has increased our understanding of women's legitimate struggle to change rape culture's very conditions. Yet, the level of sexual violence and aggression against women and girls is so vast and ubiquitous that the statistics remain staggering and massively undercounted. It includes men, boys, girls, women, transgender folks, and others who identify as non-binary.

From direct community organizing experience, there are some examples that highlight organizing culture, and how changes can be made. For example, many are found in the history of community organizing in Memphis ACORN, New Orleans ACORN and its subsequent offshoot in Louisiana, A Community Voice, as well as in Boston and national ACORN.

In 1979, the Memphis ACORN chapter began a pioneering campaign against rape by an organized community group. An incident was brought forward by a single mother, Irene Boxley, a resident in ACORN organized Section 8 apartments of North Memphis. Her differently-abled daughter was raped in a Memphis public school gym (Humes). The principal and vice-principal, both male, denied the rape, ridiculed the daughter, and ostracized the mother.

The ACORN chapter in the apartments was almost entirely women and was led by women of color, experienced in fighting issues of injustice. The mother's courage in bringing forward her own heartbreak for her daughter and the way she was dealt with were met with strong sympathy, empathy, and support for making vital changes in an institution. Her voice was supported *before* she brought the tender and hurtful subject to them. She struggled to believe that her sisters there had the fight in them and would rally with her. The leader of the group had earlier also been a member of the Welfare Rights Organization. Throughout the pickets, the shunning, the division of the principal's favorites against the ACORN members, she was strengthened and her daughter supported.

In the end, as a result of the campaign, the principal was fired, the school had new procedures, and there was security for the students. Uncharacteristically, the right-wing daily newspaper, the *Memphis Commercial Appeal,* even wrote an editorial supporting change at Humes (a heralded school in Memphis because Elvis Presley graduated from there). We also won justice and a belief in fighting for change. Participants, observers, and others learned the value of community organizing.

This wildly successful campaign presaged another rape campaign in the ACORN chapter in New Orleans. In this case, the rape was in an abandoned house. After the city failed to act, the group decided to tear down the house in a single day. The member, grandmother of the girl, asked the group to do something about the house because it represented a perpetual threat across the street from her home on Alabo Street in the now iconic lower Ninth Ward. The leader of the group, Albert Gilmore—a teacher and a member of the strong teacher's union UTNO—had also been involved in the civil rights struggles with police, fire hoses, and dogs at Southern University. He met with the organizer and together they asked the grandmother what she wanted the solution to be. She wanted the house torn down. It was a nuisance attracting such crimes.

Research turned up the elderly owner, who had moved to another state. A neighbor provided a telephone number for him. His response to the organizer was that he had no funds to tear down the house but after being told that the group was going to tear it down anyway, he said he was okay with that, and then laughed in a kind way.

Another ACORN leader, Robert Thompson from the Treme ACORN chapter, had construction skills and was asked to develop the plan to bring it down. The organizing plan was to involve the community at whatever level they could participate, and to do extensive outreach in the larger community for any women who wanted to participate in a way that would bring together the mixed-income African-American community with the whiter and gay community. The members posted flyers at women's and lesbians' bars asking them to bring their tools and help tear down the house. The members who couldn't do the physical work planned a seafood boil to serve food to the working members.

Rebecca Batiste from the local ACORN group arranged with a contact in the sanitation department to pick up the debris on the following Monday morning. The main leader for the action was a lifelong resident and social worker, Dorothy Boyd, who had been raped at the age of thirteen, and "never felt clean since then." The leadership was prepared for the inevitable challenges to the lower Ninth ward—an African-American neighborhood stigmatized as poor, black, and down and out. From the media we knew to expect the question "What were they doing for a permit to tear down a house?" Our response? "Where was the city's permit to leave a house wide open and threatening to the community? Where was the owner's permit to leave his house this way? Where was the rapist's permit to rape this girl?"

The organization in a wildly celebratory action took the house down to the ground.

The reaction by the police became far worse after ACORN leader Gilmore was quoted in a news article saying, "The police never come here. This is the area that care forgot." Immediately, regular visits began to be made to the ACORN office by the famously brutal New Orleans police who made demands to know the names of those involved in demolishing the house. Policemen even came to canvass job interviews to infiltrate and obtain the information. When their threats in the press to arrest us all didn't work, they held up the sanitation trucks from picking up the neatly piled detritus from the house teardown. Then in a pique of planned terrorism, one night they broke the very large plate glass windows in the front of the ACORN office on Baronne Street, stole three electric typewriters that were then dumped in a nearby garbage can, just to leave a message.

ACORN members lobbied the state legislature and eventually in a huge victory, the state law was changed so that a rotten house could be torn down. In the meantime, overwhelmingly women and many men from all over the city were enthused and thrilled at this fight so clearly highlighting the strength of the community and its women leaders in fighting and winning against the system. Civil rights veteran and pioneer Dorothy Mae Taylor—later the first African-American woman city council representative—recounted to the group how proud she was of them. People would approach ACORN leaders and staff to recount their own attendance at the event that day. Some of the members could only smile when so many people came forward claiming to have been involved in the teardown, since their numbers were several times that of the actual attendees.

ACORN initiated a citywide campaign (with adverse reaction from the local rape crisis center leaders) to demand a social worker be in attendance with the police when they answered the calls from sexually abused people. Al Gilmore of the lower Ninth ward chapter was also a leader in this fight and critical in teaching other members and leaders in the local group more about directly and publicly taking on the police. Gilmore endured threats after his quotes in the paper, including from the principal of his school, to whom he retorted that his "personal time was outside their bounds—check the union contract." He received offers to hide from his friends and family, but he told his local ACORN members what he had learned in his civil rights fights at Southern University, "Sometimes blood will have to be shed." Though funding was established for the social worker position, it was years before the victory was fully won.

Boston ACORN also engaged in significant, successful campaigns through more traditional community organizing work for street lights and other changes to make women safer. In post–Katrina New Orleans, A Community Voice (ACV) (formerly Louisiana ACORN) leaders Vanessa Gueringer and Gwendolyn Adams learned this history, when a student was violated in an abandoned house on an unlit street in the lower Ninth ward. They began an anti-rape campaign. After the marching and rallying, suddenly five abandoned houses on that block were torn down, all of the street lights were brilliantly relit, and the school system stopped drivers from making drop-offs in blighted areas.

Later, a woman we'll call Mary contacted ACV when chapters were working on rape issues in the low-to moderate-income neighborhoods of New Orleans. She heard that ACV members were doing outreach on a rape issue. In her initial visit it was very clear that she hadn't been listened to by authorities. The group applied pressure and negotiated with the official police monitoring group in order to get them to have the police to investigate the crime against her.

These local efforts triggered a national rape campaign by the members. ACORN joined with other organizations and was able to help lift existing campaigns and support the efforts of mainstream women's groups who led the way in proposing the National Violence Against Women Act (NVAWA). Although rape was seen as a women's issue, ACORN had been politicized and grasped the problem as a community issue, so it was normal to step into the "women's arena" and support the NVAWA through a national canvass and lobbying operation. ACORN was credited by some of the women's groups with helping the NVAWA be passed where it had previously been doomed to failure.

STUDENTS WIN LGBTQ RIGHTS AT CHARLOTTESVILLE SCHOOLS
By Joe Szakos

Campaigns start in many different ways. Sometimes a new organizing drive involves people going door-to-door, asking residents what they want to see changed in their community. Sometimes an established organization does a serious community power analysis and realizes they have the potential to have a real impact on affordable housing or a living wage. And sometimes a group of parents and students fight to get the local school board to change suspension policies that contribute to the "school-to-prison pipeline."

Then there are the times when an emerging statewide organization, like Virginia Organizing was in 1999, decides to focus on getting more young people involved in internships, learning community organizing skills, in the hopes that some of those young people might eventually be recruited as staff organizers. Danielle Poux, an early Chairperson of Virginia Organizing, convinced the organization's State Governing Board that year that in a southern state without a plethora of community organizers, internships for young people were a critical part of the change equation.

One day Brian Johns, a college student at the time, walked into the Virginia Organizing office in Charlottesville and said he wanted to learn about community organizing.

The next day, by coincidence, Lillian Ray (who now relates as Max Ray-Riek), a high school student, came into the office asking to learn how to organize for social justice.

Lillian recruited Nora Oberman (who now relates as David) and Joelle Meniktos-Nolting, fellow high school students. Since the Virginia Organizing staff's focus was to help young people learn organizing skills, they let the young interns decide what issue they wanted to tackle with a campaign.

The group decided to organize to add sexual orientation to the non-discrimination policy of the Charlottesville City Schools. Remember, at this time, the Christian Coalition was raging in Virginia, the Moral Majority was headquartered just an hour's drive away in Lynchburg, and the fight for LGBTQ rights was very different from what it is today. An attempt to add sexual orientation to the Charlottesville school policy had failed twice before—because it was framed as a legal issue, with the superintendent hyper-focused on liability. The group decided to make it a human rights issue and eventually it also became a "student safety" issue.

Mentored by an experienced community organizer, the students decided to challenge the notion that most people in the Charlottesville area were against gay rights. They soon added community members with previous civil rights experience to their strategy team, and together they decided a four-pronged approach:

1) Stockpile letters to the editor

All the members of the strategy team learned how to write letters to the editor, recruit others to write, make clear arguments, and demonstrate that there was little community opposition. The letters were literally put in a pile and one was put in the mail every other day.

2) Get public endorsements

Eventually, more than 40 groups and businesses endorsed the campaign, but the group went after the hardest ones first. For example, because local African-American organizations had been slow to endorse LGBTQ campaigns, the Charlottesville-Albemarle NAACP became a focus. Since Virginia Organizing had strongly supported the NAACP's recent anti-racism campaigns and because of strong relationships among both organizations' leaders, the local branch of the NAACP not only endorsed but became active in getting more endorsements and writing letters to the editor.

3) Meet with individual school board members with one student and one community ally

Instead of going to the school board first, the group waited until there was a lot of momentum. Letters appeared in the local paper two or three times a week for several months, and the endorsement list was steadily growing. The strategy was not just to gain support of a few key board members but to shift the frame of the issue away from a legal/liability one to make it about human rights and student safety, and to ask supportive board members to help do a more detailed power analysis of the other board members.

4) Ask the school board to take action

Momentum was strong and the group finally got the school superintendent, who was really against the policy change, to say he was "neutral" before asking the school board chairperson to put it on the agenda. With seven school board members, they needed four votes to claim victory. Very little opposition surfaced and the board looked at the issue from the students' perspective and took decisive action with a five-to-one vote.

An article in the Virginia Organizing newsletter at the time tells it all: "Led by four student interns in 1999-2000, (we) succeeded in a campaign to convince the Charlottesville School Board to add sexual orientation to the non-discrimination policy for students and employees."

After the successful Charlottesville campaign was completed, a student from adjacent Albemarle County, Adam Turner, asked for help in getting that school system to adopt the non-discrimination policy. We told Adam that we needed about 10-15 students who were willing to put in 10-15 hours a week for at least six months. Their group met and said no.

But about a year later, Adam walked into the Virginia Organizing office and said, "We are ready!" He had recruited a group of students willing to work on the campaign. Adam knew Albemarle County would be much harder than the Charlottesville campaign, so he ended up recruiting a lot more students. LaToya Brackett, who was the 32nd student to testify at the public hearing before the Albemarle County School Board voted 4-to-2 to adopt the non-discrimination policy, said boldly, "As an African-American, I was too young for the first civil rights movement, but I am not too young to miss this civil rights fight."

What other lessons did we learn?

The strategy team met every week. To participate, members had to have recruited at least one letter to the editor that week. The theme was: "If you want to be part of this campaign and sit at the table to develop the strategy, you have to do the work."

In addition to challenging the long-held belief that conservatives controlled the public space and that school boards would not want to touch LGBTQ rights issues; the campaign became a launching pad for future campaigns on LGBTQ issues and other social justice issues.

As a deliberately growing organization, Virginia Organizing had been looking for ways to include a wider range of constituencies in its statewide organizing, and the young people had scored an important victory that did just that. The clear signals about inclusivity in the non-discrimination policy campaign led to future campaigns that included the LGBTQ community from the very beginning: health care (federal and state), transgender issues (local and state), and school suspensions (local and state).

Also, the campaign to add sexual orientation to the non-discrimination policy in the schools reinforced Virginia Organizing's strategy to have local campaigns serve as an entry point for those directly affected. Organizing locally, with a time frame that allows for leadership development and political education, was also a key to future campaigns around race (data collection/racial profiling, school suspension) and class (living wage, affordable housing).

The organization committed itself to the idea that campaigns should be organized to make specific, tangible changes in people's lives; those directly affected should be the main spokespeople for the campaign. In Charlottesville, it wasn't just about getting a long list of groups to endorse the campaign. The group deliberately built relationships across constituency lines, which laid the groundwork for the development of a permanent local chapter and other local wins —getting more public housing residents to be on the housing authority board, winning gains on accessibility and mobility issues in the school system, and on local living wage campaigns.

They learned that there was more public support for LGBTQ issues than people thought—they tested this by using some tactics that extended the timeline of the campaign, which also provided more leadership development opportunities and built more strategic organizing capacity (power) for the organization. They were in no rush to ask the chair of the school board to put the issue for a vote.

They took the time to understand the strategic nature of the campaign, always asking, "Why are we doing it this way?" They wanted to do more than just change a public policy. They also wanted to add to the broader—transformational—way that LGBTQ folks were treated.

What the organization also learned from the local sexual orientation campaign was that if we are deliberate about having young people learn organizing and democratic skills, those involved will work on broader social and economic justice issues for years to come.

The college student Brian Johns is now, two decades later, Executive Director of Virginia Organizing. "This was the first time I experienced what a strategic campaign looked like," he remembers. "In short, this was the first time I witnessed power being built through grassroots organizing. I was hooked."

Max Ray-Riek also recently reflected on his participation in the campaign: "Working on the campaign without wanting to feel outed was challenging, so what was really moving about it was all of the opportunities for allies to step up and do some of the public work of the campaign. It was incredibly moving, for example, when the Public Housing Association of Residents signed on to support the campaign, noting that while they had their personal feelings about gay-ness, they had a much stronger value that no one should be targeted or made to feel unsafe, especially at school, and they knew that from their own and their kids' lived experiences of being unsafe at school."

Postscript

Max is a community activist with ACT UP Philadelphia by night, and a math educator by day. LaToya Brackett is a college professor, advocate, and activist.

IMMIGRANTS' RIGHTS STRENGTHENED IN LAWRENCE, MASSACHUSETTS
By Emily Bloch

Many of the 125,000 immigrants living in the Merrimack Valley cities of Lowell, Lawrence, and Haverhill, Massachusetts, face difficult lives because of their uncertain immigration status, and the low-wage jobs that often go with this status. With increased enforcement of immigration laws by U.S. Immigration and Enforcement (ICE), immigrants' lives are further at risk.

In Lawrence, a city of 80,000, a majority immigrant city, Merrimack Valley Project (MVP) chapter leaders decided to push their city council to pass the Massachusetts Transparency and Responsibility Using State Tools (TRUST) Act, which would prohibit the police from cooperating with ICE.

This is an account of the Lawrence chapter leaders' campaign.

MVP was organized in 1989 by regional religious, labor, and community organizations to build power for justice by uniting leaders across lines of difference—helping them develop their leadership skills and win campaigns for good jobs, affordable housing, and immigrant rights. MVP is a founding member of the InterValley Project (IVP), a New England organizing network.

We spent two months listening to people share their stories over cups of coffee in living rooms and church basements. Some talked about family members who had been deported a few months earlier for driving without a license and their fear of being stopped by the police while driving children to school. Others talked about recent break-ins, gun shots that could be heard in a park on summer nights, and slow police response time after a congregant and his nine-year old niece were stabbed walking home from services. The pain of these stories brought the community together around the shared values of family and safety but also tore it apart with seemingly different ideas what was needed to increase safety.

At first these stories were shared within pockets of people who mostly already knew each other, the Ecuadorians with the Ecuadorians, the Dominicans with the Dominicans, and the Guatemalans with the Guatemalans. But it was clear that if these stories could not be shared across communities we would hit a dead end in terms of what issues to work on.

There was tension in the room at the first organizing meeting where we brought these different groups together. A Dominican grandmother spoke about losing her son to gun violence and a Guatemalan woman shared a story about her uncle who had been stopped by local police and deported a few years earlier.

The stories in the room were real and heavy. After more relationship building, research, and deliberation, the leaders in Lawrence decided to work on passing a city council TRUST Act to end collaboration between local police and ICE, and a non-binding resolution encouraging the state legislature to pass a driver's license for undocumented immigrants.

The campaign was led by a multi-racial, multi-lingual group of MVP leaders. In early spring of 2015, along with a coalition of statewide and local groups who hoped to use Lawrence as a model that could be replicated across the state, we set out to push the nine-member city council and Mayor Daniel Rivera to agree to our demands.

We knew we only had a few months to introduce the legislation and get it passed before the city council was off for the summer. We set up meetings with the mayor and each city councilor, sending leaders to explain the issue and get a sense of who was supportive and who we needed to persuade.

Early one morning five leaders gathered in the lobby of city hall to invite Mayor Rivera to a large community forum. He committed to coming to the forum but wouldn't tell us if he would support the campaign. A few months earlier he had told an organizer at the local labor union we were working with that he would be supportive, but his reluctance to come out and publicly support made us nervous that he had changed his mind.

Agustin and I went to the local park where the Ecuadorians played volleyball and we handed out fliers, Jacqueline went from church to church on Sunday morning making announcements, and Sonia talked to everyone who came into her store about the community forum. A week later 350 people packed into the gym at St. Mary's of the Assumption. As people streamed in, the city council members that we invited took their seats in the front row. The mayor though was nowhere to be found.

After some last-minute decision-making we decided to start anyway. We heard stories from people about why this issue mattered to them, about why they had poured hours of their time into this campaign. Still Mayor Rivera had not arrived. Wilson talked about the next steps in the campaign and Jacqueline passed out surveys and asked people to sign up to get involved. Still Mayor Rivera had not arrived. Then one by one we brought forward the city council members who were there—each one pledging to support the campaign and pass the TRUST Act.

The energy in the room at this point was thick with anticipation. What would we do if the Mayor didn't show up? And just then, over an hour late, Mayor Rivera came in through the back door and with all eyes in his direction he walked up to the front of the room. In Spanish, Jacqueline and Wilson invited him to the stage, ready to ask the question if he would sign the TRUST Act and the driver's license resolution. Before they could ask the question, the mayor took the microphone, launching into a campaign speech which included a mumbled apology blaming his lateness on changing diapers and a new baby.

As Mayor Rivera droned on all the air left the room. Jacqueline looked across the stage nervously to the other leaders wondering what to do, and a few seconds later with a deep breath she grabbed the other microphone and said, interrupting him, "Mayor Rivera, thank you for coming, we have a few specific questions for you." He looked around startled and Jacqueline launched into her questions. "Mayor Rivera, will you sign a resolution encouraging the state legislature to pass a bill for driver's licenses for undocumented immigrants?"

"Yes, I care about the safety of all residents of Lawrence."

Everyone cheered and before he could restart his campaign speech Jacqueline interjected, "Mayor Rivera will you sign the Trust Act ending ICE police collaboration in the city of Lawrence?"

"No," he said, and the sense of victory that had filled the room a few minutes earlier vanished.

As the Mayor sat down Wilson stood back up, and with urgency in his voice said that it was more important than ever that people show up at the city council meeting where they would be voting on our bills.

Two weeks later the city council meeting room was packed full, with a hundred more waiting outside. Families were there with their children, construction workers in their work clothes, and community members were there in their button up shirts and church dresses waiting to share their stories and signing up to speak in public for the first time. After the speeches of support and opposition and hours of debate, the city council finally voted 7-2 to pass the TRUST Act and a resolution encouraging the state legislature to pass a bill for driver's licenses for undocumented immigrants.

Still we didn't know if that vote would hold if the mayor vetoed the bill. Leaders went again to meet with mayor, newspapers were interviewing him, and the statewide Spanish language TV news picked up the story. Still the Mayor wouldn't commit to anything, the leaders felt like he was worried that it could be used against him if he ran for higher office in a district that would include the conservative suburbs around the city.

We kept up the pressure knowing that he only had ten days to veto once the bills were passed by the city council. We had priests drop in on his office, long time community leaders make phone calls, and community members write public letters in support.

Newspaper articles were coming out every other day, everyone wanted to know if the only Latino mayor in Massachusetts was going to turn on the will of the people.

And in the end, MVP won. The mayor did not veto the bill, acknowledging the will of the people as expressed through our campaign and the vote of the council.

This campaign united the diverse immigrant community in Lawrence by helping leaders share and listen to each other's stories. It moved people into action based on direct, face-to-face contact, not just through the work of the organizer, but, more importantly, by leaders acting as volunteer organizers, in churches, workplaces, and stores. It was based on clear-cut demands, persistent and strategic pressure.

It has provided a backdrop for MVP's current Sanctuary Network campaign in which eighteen Valley urban and suburban congregations have committed to protecting undocumented immigrants from deportation by shielding them from ICE.

TAXES AND CITY SERVICES

BLOCKING THE BRISTOL COUNCIL TAX
By Nick Ballard and Anny Cullum

ACORN Bristol celebrated victory after winning our campaign forcing the Bristol City Council (BCC) to retain the Council Tax Reduction. Council Tax is a tax collected by local British authorities and used to fund public services and social care.

Many British people are critical of the regressive nature of council tax because the amount a household is expected to pay is determined by the value of the house or flat as of 1991. If the house was built after 1991 then it would be assigned a council tax 'band' of a similar sized house in the area. There are eight council tax bands—A, the lowest, up to H, the highest—and people in band A houses in Bristol are charged just over £100 per month for ten months of the year.

People on low incomes, pensions, or in receipt of certain benefits used to be eligible for Council Tax Benefit, a centrally administered benefit which was scrapped in 2013. Following this, the government passed on the administration of any council tax relief to local authorities. Since then councils have been running council tax reduction schemes through which individuals can apply for a reduction in the amount of tax they have to pay. Those on the lowest incomes were eligible for a 100 percent exemption. Unemployment benefit in the UK is around £70 per week—it would be incredibly difficult for individuals to lose £25 of that to council tax.

These reduction schemes legally have to be revisited every year by local authorities and under the economic context of austerity and further government cuts, councils across the country have opted to reduce the support they offer to low-income households by setting limits on the amount of reduction people can apply for. The most common method has been to impose a minimum charge on all households, so that everyone would have to pay, for example, at least 25 percent of the bill for their area.

Being the last major city to still maintain a 100 percent exemption policy, Bristol City Council planned to scrap this in April 2018 when the new tax year started. In the previous July, they created an online consultation which offered Bristolians three options for the council tax reduction scheme; cut, cut, or cut. Each option would have seen those on very low-incomes having to pay around £5 - £10 per week. That may not sound a lot of money to some, but when you are trying to survive on unemployment benefits, that money can be the difference between putting food on the table and heating your home.

At our July quarterly meeting, ACORN members, outraged by these proposals to take even more money from those struggling the most, voted to challenge the council's proposals and to campaign for them to keep a 100 percent reduction for people on low incomes. This was a move away from our usual focus on housing, but many members would be directly affected if the changes went ahead. In the climate of zero-hours contracts and low job security many of us could find ourselves unemployed with little warning and having to worry about paying council tax on top of everything else. It was also a conscious effort to make a move to becoming the multi-issue organization we've always intended ACORN Bristol to be.

The campaign began with members running two evening strategy sessions in August in which they conducted a power analysis, evaluated our own organizational resources, and explored the leverage we could bring to bear upon potential targets. An escalating campaign strategy was developed with direct action to coincide with key developments and dates and the decision that if necessary we would coordinate a council tax strike and defend members from eviction due to rent arrears arising from the change in policy. It was also clear that exerting pressure on the politicians through the grassroots of the ruling Labour party would be vital.

Members also identified the three most affected areas of the city in which to concentrate our organizing efforts. These also rank among the most deprived nationally: Lawrence Hill (where our offices are based and close to our heartland of Easton), Hartcliffe (an estate on the southwest edge of the city), and Lawrence Weston (an estate on the northwest edge of the city).

Making a virtue of necessity, we run an extremely tight ship, staff-wise, and instead rely on our members to take on as many traditionally staff roles as possible. Not only is this essential for our survival as an organization but it also increases the democracy and sense of ownership and investment members feel for ACORN.

Member organizers are divided into teams with a particular remit to facilitate an efficient division of labor.

Given the iron grip that centrally-imposed austerity is exercising on local government, it was clear that fighting solely on the human cost would be insufficient to sway politicians facing disastrous city finances and without the political will to mount a meaningful existence. Our campaign therefore also had to demonstrate that the proposed plans would have the opposite to intended effect and actually cost the city money. Our research team found studies confirming our belief in the false economy of these measures and that the short-term savings would increase larger problems such as homelessness, and can lead to a greater strain on public services.

A change of this sort necessitates a public consultation, a recommendation by council officers (high-level unelected council managers) to the mayor's cabinet who in turn make a recommendation to full council to vote on. The cabinet meeting was scheduled for the end of October and the council vote for December. We would need to convince dozens of councilors from the ruling party to rebel in order to win a straight vote, so our best case scenario goal was to kill off the plans before they got to that stage.

Given the time constraints dictated by the council's decision-making process, we were limited to only two weeks on the ground in each area meaning that we had to hit it hard and fast. Members were out at least three times a week between late August and early October. Taking each in turn ACORN members hustled their way into tower blocks to knock doors and held stalls outside shopping centers, schools, and other community hubs. We focused on generating 'none of the above' responses to the council's consultation and on gathering signatures on an online and offline petition to build our mandate and network.

Local meetings were organized and then mini-actions where residents and ACORN members would meet with councilors and let them know that we expected them to vote against the proposals should it come to it and work to prevent this. Largely due to time constraints, the first two public meetings were small, prompting a shift from hit-and-miss doorknocking to a centrally-located stall to both engage greater numbers and allow follow-up conversations as we became more of a fixture. This approach seemed more successful for the couple of weeks spent in Lawrence Weston, however we found out that we had won the campaign before holding the public meeting, so a full evaluation of the relative merits was not possible.

Online outreach has been a key part of our expansion in Bristol and for this campaign volunteer organizers from our communications team created videos of ACORN members explaining what the loss of income would mean for them and their families. Social media was a very important tool as it provides a very public platform, not only to spread the campaign but also to engage with councilors and apply pressure to them. Given our lack of office staff, our data team was also invaluable transferring contact details from paper to our database in short order; allowing quick email follow up and circulation of campaign updates and media content.

Our initial focus on mobilizing responses to the consultation to deny the council a mandate and a petition to build our own was very successful with the council forced to admit that 40 percent of all responses had come via ACORN and called for 'none of the above.' This, coupled with the 4,000 petition signatures gathered, made it clear where public feeling lay and who commanded it. ACORN members also organized within the Labour party to pass several supportive motions at both the constituency and ward levels, applying upward pressure on councilors and a mayor already coming under fire from their own grassroots for their lukewarm opposition to austerity.

Bristol's seventy-three seat council is comprised of the ruling Labour party with thirty-seven seats and the rest divided between the Conservatives, Greens, and Liberal Democrats. We had already secured commitments from the Greens and Liberal Democrats to vote against any changes, and we had discounted Conservative support given that they had attempted to bring in these same measures in

February. To win a council vote we would need to swing large numbers of Labour councilors and convince them to defy their mayor—no easy task as the Labour Mayor Marvin Rees had expressed public support for the proposed changes when questioned by the media. We were asking councilors to vote against their party leadership but with their wider party values.

We felt a better option would be to make the issue so politically damaging to the mayor that rather than face a public rebellion of councilors (even one with insufficient strength to win the vote outright) he would abandon the plans at the earliest possible stage.

After conducting an analysis of Labour councilors and their relative sympathy with our cause, members made plans to visit them in turn with a small delegation to demand that they support our position should the issue go to a vote. We first went after the low-hanging fruit of those most likely to rebel in order to publicize our gains and so pile on the pressure on those less ready to put their heads above the parapet. In the first week we got commitments from four councilors ready to defy the party line while the same number again committed to work behind the scenes to pressure the mayor to scrap the plans.

We were told several times that we were winning the argument among councilors but that the mayor was holding firm. A sympathetic councilor told us of an upcoming weekend retreat where the policy would be discussed and suggested we prepare a document for the councilors laying out our position. We did this, highlighting not only the economic arguments but also the incongruity of a Labour administration penalizing the poorest given the national party's rhetoric of 'For the many, not the few' and committing ourselves to exacting the maximum political cost. We circulated this widely on social media, so that no one could claim ignorance.

With twenty-four hours to go, a councilor ally and ACORN member leaked us a document prepared by the mayor's office that attempted to discredit our position and very worryingly, the result of the consultation, stating that because we had mobilized people to participate in the democratic process it had somehow become invalidated! Rather than issue a rebuttal and so endanger our source we prepped several councilors with counter-arguments and left them to it.

Allies within the council meeting indicated early on that we had successfully persuaded a majority of Labour councilors to support our position and that the mayor and his supporters had conceded defeat, agreeing to keep the scheme unchanged. This was confirmed a few days later by way of the mayor's "state of the city" address.

Our initial plans for the campaign saw us preparing to apply serious pressure in the form of a non-payment campaign or the threat of such, right up to mid-December when the vote was scheduled. As it turned out our ground-level operation, quality research, and ability to organize and apply pressure within the Labour party, combined with a willingness to take serious direct action, meant that the mayor decided the political cost was not worth battle. The end result then was ACORN's biggest UK win to date, delivered under-budget and two months ahead of schedule, and translating to up to £8 million saved for 25,000 low-income Bristolians and developing increased experience and confidence in our leadership.

LEVELING THE FIELD ON PROPERTY TAX EQUALIZATION
By Steven Kest and Wade Rathke

Property tax abuses were the focus of this long running campaign as well as the systemic faults inherent in the administration and collection of property taxes in Arkansas.

The campaign began in the spring of 1973 with the discovery of highly favorable assessments received by several Little Rock political big shots. In Pulaski County, as in most US jurisdictions, property tax records are publicly available for inspection. In the pre-Internet days this meant endless hours in the records room of the county tax assessor, but now many assessment records around the country are online.

It was decided by the ACORN board composed of all the groups in Pulaski County that the best way to make property tax reform a statewide political issue was to generate large amounts of action and publicity on obvious property tax scandals. Consequently, the opening actions of the tax campaign included a Tax Tour—ACORN members and members of the press all jammed into a bus which drove to each of the more glaring targets—and a press conference to call attention to the scandals that involved the biggest names and the largest amounts of money.

These activities were followed up by detailed exposés of the often illegal and usually unjust activities of the various county and state institutions responsible for administering property taxes. The combined impact of these media events forced county officials into the campaign once they realized there was lost revenue, forcing them to commit to reassessment of large sections of downtown Little Rock property.

ACORN members spent the rest of the 1973 tax season (the summer) holding mass actions at the county board of equalization meetings, demanding and getting meetings with the state officials in charge of taxation, and forcing a number of very important reforms in the way the board of equalization did business. Many ACORN members also filed formal appeals over their individual property assessments, flooding the office and the process.

The following year, building on the general awareness of property tax abuse that had been created in 1973, ACORN moved directly against the more far-reaching biases that were built into the way the taxing authorities interpreted the state property tax law. The staff put together a detailed study of neighborhood by neighborhood discrimination in assessments. The low-and moderate-income neighborhoods, not surprisingly, had received larger increases than the richer neighborhoods. After a series of confrontations with the Pulaski County assessor and the board of equalization, the members received a commitment that at least one of the ACORN neighborhoods (the largest and most discriminated against) would have its assessments reduced.

At the same time ACORN released a study that proved that, contrary to state law, industrial property was being taxed at a rate lower than residential property. ACORN groups once again visited the assessor and board of equalization *en masse*. The officials were not prepared to give way on this issue, however, so ACORN took the matter to the state Attorney General (AG). The AG issued a formal opinion that such disparities were unconstitutional. Eventually, the assessor caved in and undertook a total equalization review of all property in the entire county, saving lower-income owners substantial sums and proportioning industrial, commercial, and wealth properties correctly.

DON'T BE A BLOCKHEAD
By Robert Fisher, Fred Brooks, and Daniel Russell

In the spring of 2003, Wade Rathke, the founder and chief organizer of ACORN, discussed the issue of EITC (Earned Income Tax Credit) and the problem of RALs (Refund Anticipation Loans) with the Marguerite Casey Foundation. The Casey Foundation indicated interest in funding a broad initiative around EITC. Quickly ACORN's Financial Justice Center began to prepare a plan of action and a grant proposal to (1) run free tax preparation sites in three southern cities with low EITC filing rates and (2) develop a national anti-RALs campaign targeting tax preparation companies focusing on EITC recipients. H&R Block would be the first target, because it was the biggest and most prestigious. While ACORN readied to launch the direct-action campaign with or without grant funding, the Casey grant, issued in early 2004, provided the resources to run a well-funded campaign simultaneously at the national and local levels. But it offered very little start-up time. The prime time for this campaign was the 2004 tax season from January 1 through April 15.

Significantly, ACORN had experience with financial justice campaigns and was already part of a financial justice movement that targeted corporations, for example, defending the Community Reinvestment Act and opposing Household Finance around predatory lending. In their 1993 campaign against insurance redlining, ACORN targeted Allstate and held actions at sales offices in fourteen different cities. In 1994 Allstate signed an agreement with ACORN for a $10 million partnership with ACORN and NationsBank for below-market mortgages to low-income home buyers. In addition to their prior experience, ACORN benefited heavily in the campaign against H&R Block from the extensive research on RALs already done by the National Consumer Law Center, the Consumer Federation of America, and the Brookings Institution. ACORN entered an on-going struggle, equipped with a new tactic of direct action while building on the prior lawsuits and advocacy research of the on-going effort of loosely connected organizations.

The first ACORN action in the RALs campaign began in Los Angeles at the end of 2003 when twenty members held a press conference in front of the IRS building. ACORN protesters described the dangers of RALs and urged taxpayers to call ACORN to get their taxes done for free. The first nationwide action occurred on January 13, 2004. A day earlier the *Dow Jones Business News* reported, "Tax preparation giant H&R Block will come under fire Tuesday for its popular tax refund anticipation loans, as community groups launch protests planned in more than thrity U.S. cities" (Christie 2004). The protests will include "people wearing boxes on their heads saying, 'DON'T BE A BLOCKHEAD'" (Christie 2004). On the 13th, ACORN held actions at forty-three different Block offices across the nation in neighborhoods where ACORN had local chapters. They sought to get the attention of both H&R Block and the media. Critical to the effort, ACORN recorded that the actions on January 13 were covered by at least sixty-four media outlets.

On this first day of national protest, the actions at the various local events were scripted by the national campaign. In general, members went to Block offices and demanded to fax a complaint letter regarding RALs to the CEO of H&R Block. Members also chanted and handed out fliers informing Block employees as well as the public, inside and outside the office, about the problems with Block and RALs. One ACORN member described the action thusly:

> "When we do go into the office...we go in there holding up signs that ... you don't have to give them all this money.... You can get your tax return done free. And we ask that they fax a letter to the corporate office to let them know that we're against it.... Usually we have the media there so this is being aired and documented. And then when they do tell you [to leave], or they call the police...if they push at us we just back up but we don't kind of push them back or anything like that.... Our presence is intimidating enough...We just stick to the issue that we're there to represent and we just inform them and do what we have to do and then we leave (ACORN member, 2004 interview)."

In actions throughout the nation, protesters accused H&R BLOCK of "stealing from the community," engaging in "price gouging," and being a "rip off" (Steinback 2003). They wore signs in Pittsburgh saying "H&R Block Steals" (Sabatini 2004). In Chicago they accused Block of "preying on the low-income population" (Shenoy 2004). In Passaic, New Jersey, where a big lighted sign in the window of the H&R Block office on Main Avenue said "Instant Money," nine people stood outside holding handwritten signs in Spanish and English demanding refunds for people they claimed were overcharged. They criticized the "instant money" offer as "deceptive, overpriced, and unfair" (Newman 2004).

ACORN set limits on the tactics used at the actions, pursuing both a tactical preference for direct action (Jasper 1997) and a balance with other political interventions (della Porta and Diani 2006). Despite the core tactic of direct action, protest in ACORN is part of a broad tactical approach. In order to get to the bargaining table ACORN chose not to push H&R Block so hard that the company would not view them as a serious organization. As one ACORN organizer noted, "It's a question of what hurts, but doesn't so much that people won't meet and talk about signing an agreement and making some changes."

The nationally coordinated local actions continued and expanded on January 31, 2004, when hundreds of ACORN members protested at fifty-five H&R Block offices demanding that corporate officials from H&R Block meet with representatives of ACORN to negotiate an end to predatory RAL practices. According to Murray (2004), ACORN hoped "to shame Block into dealing more forthrightly with their customers." Local efforts were buttressed by the protest being orchestrated again at the national level. Atlas and Dreier (2003) argue that "ACORN's most impressive attribute" is its federated, membership structure which enables it "to work simultaneously at the neighborhood, local, state, and federal levels, so that its chapter members are always 'in motion' on a variety of issues, and so that its local organizations can link up with their counterparts around the country to change national policy on key issues that can't be solved at the neighborhood or municipal level." Furthermore, the national federated structure enhanced organizational capacity beyond the local chapters. For example, in terms of the media attention generated by the campaign, the ACORN national office not only facilitated local press releases but also helped get the issue covered by national print and television media including NBC Dateline, ABC Nightline, The News Hour with Jim Lehrer, and CBS Evening News. ACORN's ability to act on both a national and local level definitely had an impact on H&R Block. This multi-spatial approach corresponds with recent scholarship on civil life, especially Skocpol (1999, 2003), that emphasizes the benefits of membership-based efforts, which operate as active, participatory locals of a national organization.

The two national protests were supported with on-going local activism. According to ACORN's records, in the first two months of 2004, ACORN members in fifty-four cities held 402 pickets, protests and demonstrations at local H&R Block locations—successfully getting the company to the negotiating table (ACORN Annual Report 2004). Many of the locals were dogged in their efforts around RALs. But they varied in terms of the number of actions, press releases, and distributions of flyers, as well as their interest in the campaign. Combining local units in a national campaign required both organizational discipline and flexibility. Not all locals were pushed as hard to participate in the RALs campaign. Larger ACORN locals, for example in New York City, had other issues absorbing their primary energy. Not all members interviewed were excited about taking up a new issue, preferring to focus on their local issues and not shift attention and resources to the Block campaign. Nevertheless, the national organization was able to exercise discipline, especially with smaller units, through the promise of rewarding local chapters with material benefits won in any agreement with the corporate target. Discipline may seem pejorative among new social movements (Epstein 1991) but it is essential to a national campaign based on coordinated local actions. But more important than organizational discipline, the issue and campaign caught on quickly with members and local staff. "From an organizer's perspective when I was [first] briefed on this campaign I was like, taxes? Oh that's so unexciting. How do we move people on taxes? [But as it turned out] it was pretty exciting [and] our members, I mean, they get it.... They understand when they're ripped off" (ACORN staff, 2004 interview). ACORN members we interviewed generally understood as well the value of protest tactics. As one member put her learning process,

> "What I like about ACORN is the direct approach, the action. Sometimes I didn't completely understand, like why don't they just talk to the people. Well, I've learned that being a member of ACORN that they have reached out and tried to talk with people that we have some issues with and they just completely ignore us. And so the one thing that we have as citizens, especially just regular working class citizens, we have the power to get with other people and just go out there and have demonstrations and actions. At first I didn't think they'd get anything done but it worked because people, especially in Indianapolis, they really don't like to be embarrassed like that (ACORN member, 2004 interview)."

Campaign outcomes

While any evaluation of campaign outcomes is mediated by the brevity and temporal proximity of ACORN's campaign, our study reveals initial results in five outcome areas: local ACORN chapters, ACORN members, ACORN as a national organization, H&R Block, and the broader financial justice campaign against Block's use of predatory RALs. (It is too soon to evaluate impacts in a sixth though critical area, the proliferation and cost of RALs especially to EITC recipients.) Regarding the local chapters, the nationally coordinated campaign with its national days of action, despite occasionally posing challenges to local chapters, had a synergistic impact. Even organizers in more established locals, where the RALs campaign had to compete with other on-going issues, spoke to the power of the national campaign and the opportunity afforded by having the national provide directions for more actions. "We can't have enough actions. They're critical to the organization. Actions strengthen people's commitment to the organization" (ACORN staff, 2004 interview). Another staff person remarked, "The RALS campaign has made us stronger in a lot of areas in terms of membership, bringing membership together, bringing new members in that we wouldn't have had if it had not been for this" (ACORN staff, 2004 interview). The social movement literature concurs. Protest tactics provide important internal functions, among them creating a sense of collective identity and building solidarities critical to action towards a common goal (Rochon 1998).

In terms of member development, our interviews, focus groups, and participant observation revealed results counter to prevailing perspectives on community building. Recent literature on community-based organizations emphasizes the importance of community building approaches to resident empowerment and education and critiques protest tactics for failing to build significant identity and solidarity networks among participants (Boyte 2004; Fabricant and Fisher 2002). Conflict strategies, especially ones developed outside the community, are said to do a poor job of participant education and development. The case study reveals more mixed initial results. As a staffer noted, "We had members who, at the beginning of their three months were like 'What's a RAL?' At the end [of the three months, they] stand up in front of a group of members and talk about RALs way better than I could. That wasn't because we did teach-ins or anything. We did a ton of actions ... people love it" (ACORN staff, 2004 interview). At their best, ACORN actions seek to move the target, in this case H&R Block, and educate the community. In terms of member education and engagement, we observed that while some participants were personally affected by RALs, most were not. The campaign often took community residents beyond personal concerns to consider larger issues within their communities, the economy, and public policy. RALs were not "just hurting individual families," one articulate member noted, "but our entire economy because this is money that could be filtered back into our communities" (ACORN member, 2004 Focus Group).

Regarding its impact on ACORN as a national organization, almost everyone interviewed was very positive about the speed of the campaign, the extent of media attention, the engagement of the locals and membership, and the resources it brought to ACORN. Overall, from ACORN's perspective, a well-orchestrated and coordinated national campaign of direct action empowered staff and members, strengthened the organization, and moved a Fortune 500 company to negotiate and support ACORN's work in poor and low-income communities. As ACORN put it in their annual report (2004):

> "Thousands of ACORN members across the country have been actively engaged in this campaign around increasing EITC and combating RALs, have discussed it in meetings, with their neighbors, and participated in actions. The H&R Block focus in specific has provided a powerful experience of participating in local actions, around problems facing your own neighborhood, but through coordination with similar actions taking place around the country, achieving a level of collective power sufficient to quickly force a major corporation to the table. Block's representative made this point in front of the 2,000-plus ACORN members gathered at the convention when he commented in his speech announcing the partnership that ACORN's activities had accomplished what years of reports and papers had never done in moving the company to make change."

Regarding its impact on H&R Block, while overall it is too soon to tell, some things are certain. Linder (2004) reported 1.2 percent fewer RALS in January 2004, than a year before, resulting from increased attention and changed practices. Roth (2004b) reported a decline in RALs sold by Block from 4.61 million the year before to 4.26 million in 2004. More directly, the campaign reaped a nearly instant response from the giant of the commercial tax preparation industry, a powerful multi-national corporation. By early February, within a month of the first protest, H&R Block and ACORN were negotiating. As noted earlier, Block was taken off guard by the January 13 action. "When it started there was a bit of a scramble here.... Once the protests started we were up to speed fairly quickly, but really it wasn't anything we were prepared for. Not something like that. Not protests at our door" (H&R Block executive, 2005 interview). Roth (2004a) concurs. "ACORN caught the company's attention when it staged January 13 demonstrations at Block tax offices in thirty cities." That day H&R Block issued a public relations statement in their local newspaper "listing the steps the Kansas City company has taken to benefit low-income taxpayers" (Roth 2004a). A few days later Block's vice president of community outreach and business development made a public announcement noting, "We recognize our low- and moderate-income clients need financial education and financial literacy support" (Davis 2004). In private discussions within the company H&R Block decided early on to meet with ACORN. They admitted to being vulnerable to bad publicity during the tax season, said they were impressed with the scope of ACORN's actions, and concluded that ACORN was a legitimate representative of low-income community residents. A Block official, sounding as though he had read Skocpol (1999, 2003), distinguished between Washington, DC-based national advocacy organizations, which he saw as without real legitimacy, and membership-based organizations such as ACORN:

> "Well, I don't think anyone ever engaged us quite the way that ACORN did...We've been engaged in the past by essentially interest groups. ACORN by contrast was a membership-supported organization principally and last year ACORN had people out there for four hundred office protests, by people who look a lot like our clients...ACORN was the first of its type to engage us and it was a more credible, more convincing engagement. They know what they are talking about because they've lived it.... ACORN, by pounding on the door so to speak, got us to listen a little bit more carefully to our client's perspective (H&R Block executive, 2005 interview)."

In addition, Block concluded rather quickly, based on a canvass of other companies that had been targeted by ACORN, that they could negotiate with ACORN (H&R Block executive, 2005 interview).

ACORN saw a direct relationship between the speed of negotiating with Block and the national action campaign of ACORN. As a staffer put it: "They've been actually much easier to get to the table to negotiate than have been other targets, you know, big banks, or finance companies, like Household Finance" (ACORN staff, 2004 interview). Wade Rathke, founder and chief organizer of ACORN, concurred, emphasizing H&R Block's exposure to a well-timed, nationwide,  direct action campaign in communities where both ACORN and Block had offices and therefore where Block was a visible and accessible target for ACORN members and community residents. "Their vulnerability to what we were doing was extremely intense and they knew it and were worried about it and responded very carefully because of that and it was the action profile and the aggressiveness of the campaign that was allowing us to move to negotiations so quickly" (Rathke, 2005 interview). Our research suggests a variety of factors that moved Block to negotiate including Block's temporal vulnerability, changes in the market for RALs, Block's desire to serve its consumer base more effectively, the work of consumer advocacy groups and legal initiatives which contributed to Block's vulnerability, ACORN's ability to disrupt Block's business operations at a local and national scale, as well as ACORN's reputation as reasonable once at the bargaining table.

The results of the negotiations were announced at the ACORN national meeting on June 28 in Los Angeles. "ACORN announced a three-year alliance with Block to help low-to mid-income people better understand tax law," according to Roth (2004). "Block officials have declined to say how much they will invest in the program…

Block will provide expertise and money to develop educational materials about tax credits and other tax saving mechanisms. ACORN will implement the program through its offices in sixty-five U.S. cities." The agreement has six main components: First, Block would help ACORN, through monetary contributions of an as yet undisclosed amount, to do work in their communities around EITC outreach. This would fund a tax literacy and assistance campaign, including information and assistance on EITC and RALs. It would be national in scope; include door-to-door outreach, education, and tax preparation services; and be based in communities where ACORN has local chapters ("H&R Block and ACORN partner" 2005). Second, Block would completely eliminate within the next two years the administrative application fee for RALs which averages $32 nationally. This is the handling fee H&R Block had already eliminated in thirteen states and the District of Columbia. ACORN estimates the value of this savings to be approximately $192 million annually, primarily to poor and low-income people and EITC recipients. They calculate that if prior research estimated $1 billion of EITC funds being lost on RALs, now nearly $200 million, or one-fifth that sum, will stay with EITC recipients. Third, ACORN won a pledge from Block to hire and educate ACORN members to be tax preparers, something that may have seemed less significant to national staff but was highly valued by members returning to their communities with the promise of lowered fees, investment, and new job opportunities. Fourth, H&R Block will provide clearer information to their customers on RALs disclosures and advertising. The language of the disclosure is meant to be as simple as possible so someone does not have to have a great deal of banking knowledge in order to realize that they are about to take out a loan. Fifth, H& R Block agreed to a rebate to ACORN members of $25 off tax returns filed during the month of March for the next three years. Sixth, ACORN agreed to cease and desist in their protests against H&R Block.

Third-party consumer advocates, prior participants in the overall effort against predatory RALs, spoke strongly to the contribution ACORN made to the movement against H&R Block. "It definitely made all the difference to have people standing in front of a Block office with signs that say, "you guys are making predatory loans….

We could write all the reports and issue press releases we want but Block cares about its image and the idea of people standing outside their offices with protest signs, I think was pretty effective" (Consumer Advocate, 2004 interview). Singletary (2005) agreed, pointing out that ACORN's addition to the anti-RALs campaign, after years of pressure from other groups "improved how they [commercial tax preparers] promote, sell, and disclose the terms of refund loans." Consumer advocates clearly supported ACORN's contribution to the RALs campaign, but always situated their evaluation of ACORN's work in the broader movement against predatory RALs. "I think it is all the different tools trying to get to the same thing…the research, the reporting, the congressional advocacy, the state level legislative advocacy, the direct action in front of the stores, the direct intervention with the companies trying to move them" (Consumer Advocate, 2005 interview).

ACORN's work must be contextualized in the broader anti-RALs campaign; to view its campaign as the sole agent of change would decontextualize ACORN's efforts and miss the complex structure and processes of social movements. Without the prior efforts which disclosed and framed the problem, legitimated and publicized the issue, and attacked and hurt Block, it is highly unlikely there would have been an ACORN campaign on RALs, let alone one that brought Block to the bargaining table so quickly.

While in general highly supportive of ACORN's contribution, part of the ambivalence of some consumer advocates relates to the secrecy surrounding aspects of the agreement between H&R Block and ACORN. We assume that ACORN is open to having all the elements of the agreement made public but did not push Block on this because, among other reasons, Block opposed it and ACORN wanted to move on to their secondary tax preparation targets such as Jackson Hewitt and Liberty Tax. We presume H&R Block opposed making public the monetary transaction in order to avoid being seen as vulnerable to protests such as ACORN's. How well an alliance will succeed based on these shaky beginnings—being forced to the bargaining table, keeping aspects of the alliance agreement secret—remains to be seen.

Even with its limits as a modest case study, our research reveals some of the potential of protest tactics as practiced in a national and community-based organization such as ACORN. Evaluations of comparable campaigns come to a similar conclusion. For Taylor and Silver (2003), their study of the Community Reinvestment Act revealed that "Activism is not passé; it is essential. Without activism, our society becomes less democratic and less just. This is true in many arenas, but especially in the fight for economic justice and equal access to credit and capital." Squires (2003) and others concur. Dreier (2003) in his analysis of predatory lending concludes that "The twenty-first century will certainly see a growing concentration of power in a smaller and smaller number of financial services conglomerates, which will present daunting challenges…. Only groups that have a national base such as ACORN… will have any reasonable chance to challenge the financial services giants." Hartman (2004), preferring federal policy initiatives, applauds ACORN's work around the earlier campaign against Household Finance for predatory lending but wonders whether they will be able to find the resources to mount it nationally and whether "confrontational tactics will produce a backlash." Perhaps it already has. As a senior vice president from Bank of America put it: "I don't want to hear one more community group tell me something negative and then ask me for $400,000 a week later. That doesn't work anymore" (Hartman 2004).

Hartman and others are correct. Addressing economic exploitation ingrained in the sub-prime financial markets and contemporary forms of unregulated capitalism will require more than community organizing or the campaign of a single organization, even a national one. ACORN is working in coalitions with other groups advocating for federal and statewide RALs legislation, with some modest recent successes in Connecticut and California. Like most of the large community organizing networks, ACORN prefers, when it has enough clout, to work autonomously, but increasingly in ongoing campaigns that ACORN joins, such as the RAL campaign, or in campaigns where they seek to have greater impact, such as living wage initiatives or electoral efforts, they increasingly work with other groups.

This case study should encourage theoreticians, researchers, and practitioners to reconsider the choice of protest tactics in community-based organizations as a means of moving vulnerable targets, drawing public attention to neglected issues, building the organization, and mobilizing and sustaining membership. It should also direct attention to the impact of adding protest tactics to existing campaigns; our research reveals direct action was an addition that complemented rather than undermined other tactical repertoires.

This case study should also encourage an increased examination of ACORN by those interested in urban social movements and community-based initiatives. Unlike most current community-based efforts, ACORN has a broader perspective that seeks, as Koehler and Wissen (2003) put it in a broader discussion of urban social movements, to "fight the destructive influences which neoliberal globalization exerts on everyday life" and politicize these contradictions through organized "urban social conflict." ACORN would not use that language, but they understand the power of multinational corporations under contemporary economic globalization, and that it requires a broad scale of activism, at least a national organization that can hold actions in more than fifty cities as they did with Block. Their strategy to target large corporations, not public agencies or officials, reflects ACORN's understanding of the shift in power and resources under contemporary policies away from the public sector in general and city officials in particular (Weir, Wolman and Swanstrom 2005). Moreover, ACORN's local as well as national capacity capitalizes on the virtues and helps transcend the limits of small scale, community activism while at the same time addressing some of the key dilemmas inherent in centralized, large scale advocacy organizations (Dreier 2003; Atlas 2005). Moreover, the national structure complements their protest tactics. If ACORN was embedded solely in a single community with a focus solely on that community, not looking beyond community borders for either causes or solutions to local problems, then ongoing protest tactics within the community—what Jane Mansbridge called "adversarial democracy"—would prove counterproductive. But in a national organization focused on both local and national campaigns, in which its broader practice and focus make it less limited by community values or long-term relationships, in which they encourage an understanding that community problems are almost always the result of policies and politics from outside the community, in an organization that probably fights more for the general interests of poor and low-income people than it does the specific interests of individual community members, protest tactics, in combination with other approaches, can work well.

SAVE THE CITY CAMPAIGN: Winning Centennial Park in Little Rock
By Steven Kest and Wade Rathke

Local ACORN groups working on local issues are crucial to what ACORN is and does. It makes sense, therefore, to look in some detail at how a particular group goes about working on an issue.

A couple of residents of Little Rock's predominately black Centennial neighborhood, which surrounds historic Central High School, were concerned about neighborhood traffic problems and spent some time in early 1972 trying to get the city of Little Rock to put up a traffic light. Rebuffed by the bureaucracy, the residents decided that they might have more success if they joined in building a larger community organization with ACORN. One of the residents had been active in other ACORN activities, and he provided a natural link to the organization. The initial group of residents plus some of their friends developed into the neighborhood organizing committee while working with a local ACORN organizer. By August, 1972, a meeting of 100 people founded the Centennial Neighborhood Association (CNA) affiliated with ACORN.

Although the traffic light was the initial local issue, another issue came to the forefront during the organizing process and rose to prominence in the first meeting. Several members had heard that the old Centennial School property in the area, then being razed, was going to be developed into either a grocery store or an apartment building. The group felt that either option would only add to the already deteriorating traffic situation in the area, as well as make their children's playground (the street!) even more hazardous than it already was. Turning the property into a park would solve both problems at once, the group quickly realized, and a park committee was formed to see what could be done.

The group circulated a petition in the neighborhood, and then arranged a meeting with the owner of the property, the Little Rock School Board. They were told by the school superintendent that perhaps the city could be persuaded to buy the property and develop the park.

Armed with 400 signatures on the petition, thirty CNA members showed up at the next meeting of the city Board of Directors. The group, having received help researching the issue from the organizer and from ACORN's research department, presented several arguments to the Board. First, they argued the Planning Commission's 1971 Master Park Plan called for several parks in the CNA area, but all the sites had homes on them. They also pointed out that the site ACORN proposed was within three blocks of two of the sites in the park plan, and was the only feasible location. They reminded the board that the CNA neighborhood contained 400 children of age fourteen or younger and the park would be a safeguard against neighborhood deterioration. Finally, they argued that the site without a park would no doubt be zoned for multi-family residential or commercial use and thus add to the neighborhood's traffic congestion.

The city was noticeably unsympathetic. One director suggested using a park a mile distant; the city manager claimed that the city had no money.

The group followed up on two fronts. First, they attended several school board meetings in order to convince the school board not to sell the land to a developer. Secondly, the group directed the organizer to find out whether the city actually did have the money, and, if it didn't, whether there was any federal or state money available to buy and develop the park. In November 1972, the CNA members succeeded in forcing the city directors to apply for a $100,000 HUD "Open Space Land Act" grant, and therefore were able to convince the school board to hold on to the land until the HUD grant was determined and succeeded.

With victory in sight, however, President Richard Nixon impounded the HUD park money. A CNA formed solely to win a park might have fallen apart while waiting for new federal money to be made available, but CNA/ACORN had plenty of other issues to keep it busy. The traffic light still had to be won (it was soon thereafter), and various citywide campaigns required the group's involvement: a fight against the Wilbur Mills Expressway, which was heading right through the old residential center of town; a campaign against a gas rate increase; and an attempt to ensure an equitable distribution of the new General Revenue Sharing funds. The last issue provided CNA with the handle it needed to finally win its park. In March 1974, the group successfully pressured the city into appropriating $85,000 of the GRS money for the acquisition and development of the park. Centennial Park now sits in the middle of the neighborhood—a real symbol to the residents of what organization can achieve.

LAND AND RESOURCES

FIVE COUNTRIES ALLIED AGAINST LAND-GRABBING
By Eloise Maulet

Farmers and residents in Cameroon, Cambodia, Liberia, Ivory Coast, and Sierra Leone are struggling together against the abuses and broken promises of agro-industrial plantations owned by a European corporation. For decades, these local communities have been affected by tensions with regard to land and the fundamental rights of farmers; pollution; disrespect for agreements; and repression.

These problems have come at the hands of palm oil and rubber tree plantations owned by Socfin, a transnational corporation based in Luxemburg. The Bolloré Group (France) owns 38.75 percent of Socfin and Bolloré is among the 500 biggest companies in the world. Its main activities are transport, logistics, communications, and energy storage, which they conduct around the world, but especially in Africa.

One of Socfin's main activities is the management of common shares from more than 181,000 hectares of tropical palm oil and rubber plantations that are located in Africa and Southeast Asia. Throughout the years, the surface area of these plantations has significantly increased. Between 2010 and 2014, the total surface area of the plantations grew from 104,424 to 181,369 hectares, representing a 29 percent increase in four years. These land expansions, experienced as land-grabs by local communities, provoke significant conflicts with the communities, as their living conditions worsen. The increasing number of unfulfilled promises by management is also fueling tensions with local communities and farmers. These people have been protesting against setting-up conditions of these plantations.

Membership organizations were created in Cameroon, Ivory Coast, Liberia, Sierra Leone, and Cambodia to defend the interests of local communities as they confront this company. With the support of ReAct organization and with ACORN as a partner, they gathered in an international alliance to coordinate the struggle and share information and experiences. The objective is to unite with sufficient power to pressure this huge multinational corporation.

From 2010 to 2012, ReAct organizers made several trips to the plantations to share collective organizing methods with local communities. The goal was to overcome division, and the corruption of certain traditional leaders and local administrative authorities, and to relieve the general sense of powerlessness. By identifying local leaders and supporting the creation and reinforcement of strong democratic local organizations, the plantation residents were able to organize themselves and seek out power collectively and consequently take a position as legitimate and representative actors.

In 2013, after exchanges between the residents' organizations from all five different countries, the Alliance of Socfin-Bolloré Plantation Residents was officially created bringing together organizations from Cameroon, the Ivory Coast, Liberia, Sierra Leone, and Cambodia. The Alliance decided to write their first letter of demands. In order to deliver the demands to Vincent Bolloré, the company CEO, they decided to organize a global day of action the day of the corporate General Assembly held in Paris.

On June 5, 2014, organized communities represented in the Alliance all took action at the same time throughout all of their countries. In Sierra Leone, several hundred villagers occupied the land of the SAC plantation. In the Ivory Coast, a peaceful march of residents was blocked by police forces as they approached the main factory and the administrative offices to deliver their message to the management of the SoGB plantation. In Douala, Cameroon, 200 farm workers and traditional leaders walked to the Socapalm plantation headquarters in their traditional mourning clothing, to symbolize the loss they were suffering.

In Paris, people from Cameroon, the Ivory Coast, and other affected countries occupied the Bolloré Group's headquarters. They carried watering cans, hand shovels, and rakes, and started tending the land outside. "We don't have any more land in our country, so we have to plant manioc in your yard!" exclaimed a man from a village in Cameroon who was directly affected by the plantations' activities.

The demands were the same from Cameroon to Sierra Leone:

- Land must be given back to guarantee the provision of a sufficient critical space for agriculture workers in their village; and,

- Fair compensation must be given for the removal of land and forests, in the form of infrastructure, social services, and support to village plantations.

In response to ongoing pressure from the Alliance members, the Bolloré Group agreed to meet with representatives from the residents' organizations. The first transnational negotiation took place in Paris on October 24, 2014. Bolloré agreed to an independent property and land assessment to shed light on the land conflicts and agreed to meet the following year in order to track progress. It was also specifically agreed that representatives from Socfin would attend the follow-up meeting, as they ignored the Alliance's demand that they appear at the first meeting.

In 2015 several transnational solidarity actions were organized to protest the arrest of organization leaders in Liberia and Sierra Leone.

The negotiation timeline was not respected. Bolloré did not involve Socfin and Socfin continued to refuse to enter into any dialogue. This sparked a new series of actions between April and June of 2015 including: peaceful protests in the plantations of Djbombari and Mbongo in Cameroon; a march to the LAC plantation management offices in Liberia; a sit-in in Cambodia; and a workers' assembly in the Ivory Coast. These actions led to renewed local negotiations in Cameroon, Liberia, and Cambodia. Tripartite platforms were set up for negotiations to take place in Cameroon and Cambodia between the company, local authorities, and communities. Bolloré Group reiterated its promise to "do everything in its power to have Hubert Fabri [the General Manager of the Socfin] participate in an international negotiation."

During the following year, there was ongoing dialogue in Cambodia, Liberia, and Cameroon, but negotiations were difficult and there were very few results on the ground. In Sierra Leone, Alliance leaders experienced repression, and for several leaders, court appearances replaced dialogue.

Management slowed down negotiations in Cambodia and Liberia, and refused to include the local community organization (Synaparcam) in the dialogue, so the results did not meet peoples' demands. In spite of this unsatisfactory response to the conflicts, Bolloré Group drew back behind Socfin, saying that "considerable sums of money are spent every year," and congratulating the "intensification of dialogue." Both Bolloré and Socfin asserted that the negotiations must remain at the local level to solve the problems.

Local communities struggled hard to get concrete results in each country. They had to go through new non-violent direct actions again in Liberia and Cameroon (occupations, student actions, sit-ins) to barely win weak promises. Reactions from local management showed that they are not ready for real negotiations with the people directly affected by land grabs or their legitimate representatives.

But the different organizations of the International Alliance of Local Communities will have a strong assessment of the dialogue and concrete results, and will continue to bring to light the local management's ill will. Socfin and Bolloré will be called out again to take responsibilities. Pressure will be renewed on the Group again at the international level if they refuse an international negotiation that would achieve significant results for people. An international coalition was able to put pressure on Socfin and Bolloré during their 2016 General Assemblies in June, and the coalition will be strengthened in Europe and wherever possible.

Postscript

- 2016: Ongoing dialogue in Cambodia, Liberia, and Cameroon, but difficult negotiations and very few results on the ground. In Sierra Leone, the repression, with several leaders in Court, is replacing the dialogue.

Management is slowing down negotiations in Cambodia and Liberia, and refuses to include the Local Communities Organization (Synaparcam) properly in the dialogue in Cameroon (only a few meetings organized in three of the seven plantations). The results thus did not comply with people's demands, despite few results on the ground. In spite of this unsatisfactory response to the conflicts, Bolloré draws back behind Socfin, saying that "considerable sums of money are spent every year," and congratulating the "intensification of dialogue." Both Bolloré and Socfin are asserting that the negotiations must remain at the local level to solve the problems.

In December 2017, the Chief of Staff of Sierra Leone Government finally committed to conduct a mediation on land use conflict in the Pujehun district, under national and international pressure from civil society, giving some hope for the opening of a constructive dialogue.

Local communities have thus been struggling hard to get concrete results in each country. They had to go through new non-violent direct actions again in Liberia and Cameroon (occupations, students actions, sit-in) to barely win weak promises.

Local communities asking for electrification in Mbambou, Cameroon, June 1, 2016

Kids "sing-in" to access school facilities in LAC, Liberia, October 5, 2016

Diasporas from Africa and activists in Paris in front of the General Assembly of Bolloré, June 3, 2016

Demonstration against Bolloré abuses in Paris: journalists, activists from France and Africa walking together, November 19, 2016

- **2017: unilateral commitments from Socfin**

After local and international pressure from local communities' organizations and from a coalition of NGOs, Socfin had to move forward and commit unilaterally (without recognition of local organizations as a negotiating partner) to certain reforms in plantation management. The Group announced a "Responsible Management Policy," with a timeline for action and specific indicators including village relationship procedures and plantation land use. Socfin defined Cameroon as the first country to target with this action plan. Socfin's commitments are thus verifiable. However, it took one more year for Socfin to start implementing its action plan.

Local communities continued to take action in Liberia and Cameroon to push local managements to meet some demands. This allowed some progress on the ground, such as access to school in LAC (Liberia) and the creation of a government commission to investigate the land conflict in Cameroon. International pressure continued with several actions in Switzerland, Luxembourg, Belgium, and France, and an increase of investigations, reports, and articles from NGOs and journalists.

- **2018: Follow-up on commitments, strengthening local organizations and legal battle**

In 2016, Socfin brought charges against two NGOs (ReAct and Sherpa) and three major French newspapers (*Mediapart*, *Le Point*, *L'Obs*). The trial took place in January 2018 in Paris and Socfin's loss was a publicity failure for the Group. But winning in court is not the point for Socfin/Bolloré. The goal is to silence criticism by imposing ruinous financial pressure on its enemies: win or lose in court, the threat of heavy legal costs can silence journalists and weaken the work of NGOs. Over the past ten years, Bolloré's cluster of corporations has brought defamation cases twenty times against journalists and NGOs.

However, legal action cuts both ways. In a major setback for the reputation of his Group, Vincent Bolloré is currently targeted by French government prosecutors for corruption in African ports that his group manages. Hubert Fabri, head of Socfin, has been brought to trial in Belgium for tax fraud and, along with other administrators of Socfin, has been charged with active corruption.

The international campaign has succeeded in optimizing French media coverage on a complex of social, legal, and environmental issues surrounding the African Palm Oil plantations of Socfin and the Bolloré Groups.

Throughout 2018, some NGOs of the coalition are focused on controlling Socfin commitments:
- locally in Cameroon, to conduct field studies, survey residents and employees, map and document disputed areas
- nationally and internationally, to pursue actions and communicate widely.

Capacity building continues with local communities to build strong and independent organizations which can continue the struggle on the long run.

On the ground, activists are verifying that management at each Socfin plantation is actually doing what was promised. Among the key points:
- Is Socfin local management really involving stakeholders in the process as pledged?
- Is a complaint procedure implemented? Does it work?

- Has planting new lands stopped pending solving of land conflicts?
- Are the maps technically correct as to boundaries? Have plantation limits—based on maps published by Socfin—enabled the return of lands to the village economies?
- Has Socfin respected the "no new deforestation" commitment?
- Has Socfin management established local procedures for discussions between their plantations and local small farmers cultivating palms?

New actions are also being taken to increase leverage for negotiations on Bolloré/Socfin on major clients (Michelin) and on major funders (banks such as ING).

Corporate research is being developed on the case to identify new paths of leverage.

NOT ON MY FIELDS AND NOT FROM MY POCKETBOOK: The White Bluff Power Plant Campaign
By Wade Rathke and Steven Kest

In September 1973, the Arkansas Power and Light Company (AP&L, now a division of Entergy) announced plans to build the gargantuan 2,800 megawatt coal-burning White Bluff power plant near Redfield, Arkansas, between Little Rock and Pine Bluff. At close to a billion dollars, the plant was to have been the single largest private investment ever undertaken in the state of Arkansas.

Were electricity the only product of the plant, Redfield citizens might have been persuaded. The plant, however, was going to turn out 178,000 tons of sulfur dioxide damage, and AP&L had no plans to install sulfur dioxide pollution controls on the plant.

As rumors of potential pollution levels began spreading, local citizens grew apprehensive and angry. The Jefferson County Improvement Organization (JCIO), an ACORN affiliate near

Redfield, whose previous focus had been the poor conditions in local schools, asked the organization for help in discovering more about AP&L's plans for Redfield. ACORN's research department discovered that the plant would turn out more than enough pollution to cause damage to crops that the area around Redfield depended on for its economic well-being.

The ACORN board, composed of members of all affiliated groups in the state, decided to authorize a full-scale organizing effort in the area. With initial help from JCIO members, ACORN began organizing hundreds of farmers in the Plum Bayou, Ferda, Tucker, Wright, and England areas into two new ACORN affiliates: the Protect Our Land Association and Save Health and Property. Meanwhile, ACORN released the results of its research in a report to the Public Service Commission (PSC), and forced the long dormant state pollution and environmental agencies to begin taking a closer look at the proposed power plant.

Back in the countryside, the now highly organized and irate farmers began to directly confront the utility company. A request delivered by a delegation of ACORN farmers and signed by more than 1,000 area residents asked the company for a $50 million "deposit in reverse." The deposit would serve as a guarantee against any damages suffered by the farmers from the plant's operation. AP&L, of course, refused to put up the deposit.

AP&L countered with an intensive public relations effort designed to prove that the plant would "help build Arkansas." ACORN responded by pointing out that the decision to build the plant had nothing to do with the needs of Arkansas; that the decision had been made by AP&L's corporate owners in the New York offices of Middle South Utilities (now Entergy). ACORN members hammered away at this point, for AP& had long enjoyed a reputation as a benevolent local company—especially in rural areas of the state, where the electric lights were first turned on within the memory of most adult farmers.

The appeal to the farmers' latent populism proved to be extremely successful, especially when the ACORN members dramatized the point by writing a letter to Middle South's largest single shareholder—Harvard University. They demanded that the University do an independent economic and environmental study of the plant's impact, and that Harvard use its leverage as the largest stockholder to pressure Middle South on the question of sulfur dioxide controls. ACORN sent an organizer to Harvard and lined up a coalition of about twenty student groups to support the farmers' demands. When Arkansas Governor Dale Bumpers spoke at Harvard that fall, he encountered stiff questioning from our supporters in the audience about politics back home, since our campaign had become front page news in the *Harvard Crimson*, the student newspaper. Bumpers responded by calling for responsible measures by AP&L to protect Arkansas from pollution and endorsed ACORN's efforts. The Arkansas press, aided by ACORN, picked up the news item and carried it across the state.

Harvard responded to the pressure by underwriting a fact-finding report by the Investor Responsibility Research Center in Washington, DC On the strength of the report, the student-faculty-alumni Advisory Committee for Shareholder Responsibility asked the Harvard corporation to support ACORN's demands. The corporation

eventually wrote a letter to Middle South urging the installation of the pollution controls.

Back in Arkansas, AP&L made one last try to capture favorable headlines before the start of the upcoming PSC hearing. Chartering a plane, AP&L invited a number of ACORN's farmers, ACORN's chief organizer, several state officials, and the press on a tour of several coal burning power plants, in order to convince everyone of the plant's harmlessness. The trip backfired, however, when ACORN found out that one of the plants on the itinerary in Kentucky was violating federal pollution standards daily, and that another had just installed pollution controls. ACORN members distributed leaflets to that effect on the plane. AP&L lost its chance for a public relations coup, prompting one official to remark that every time they were in the public eye with ACORN, "they lost."

By this time ACORN's groups had intervened in the PSC (Public Service Commission) hearings. With the assistance of an environmental lawyer from Washington and several pollution experts, ACORN and its farmer members managed to convince the commission to cut the plant's size in half (down $500,000,000). In addition, the commission reserved the right to order AP&L to install sulfur dioxide scrubbers at any time during the plant's construction if the commission were to determine the scrubbers were feasible.

DEVELOPMENT AND COMMUNITY BENEFITS

EQUITABLE DEVELOPMENT COMES TO DC
By Dominic T. Moulden and Gregory D. Squires

Equitable development has become a buzzword in urban revitalization debates as community organizations across the US pursue alternatives to traditional market-oriented, developer-driven projects. Rather than focusing on profit maximization and returns to investors, these initiatives target a triple bottom line: the interests of the business community including the needs of local employers, fairness in the treatment of employees, and sustainability to protect and enhance the resources (human and others) in responding to an array of social and environmental needs of cities. With the assistance of progressive advocacy research organizations like PolicyLink in Oakland, Demos in New York City, and Good Jobs First in Washington, DC, these urban redevelopment activities address the mutual concerns of employers, employees, and the environment. Organizing Neighborhood Equity DC (ONE DC), serving the District's Shaw neighborhood, has become one of the most concrete manifestations of the burgeoning equitable development movement in the US.

Shaw has become a very hot real estate market in Northwest DC in recent years. Located north of M Street and south of Florida Avenue between North Capital and 7th, Shaw was a center of DC's Black Renaissance from the 1920s through the 1940s—where Duke Ellington, Langston Hughes, and other notable African-Americans lived. The violence and civil disobedience of the 1960s cost the community many of its businesses and residents and few chose to move into the area for decades. But in the nineties, Shaw, like many other neighborhoods close to downtown central business districts in cities across the country, began to see an influx of new residents, many of whom did not look like most current or former residents.

Since 1990 the black population of Shaw dropped from 89 percent to 54 percent of neighborhood residents as the share of whites grew from 6 percent to 28 percent. Hispanics increased their share from 3 percent to 8 percent while the Asian population grew from

2 percent to 7 percent. Not only is the population paler, it is becoming richer. Median family income grew from $21,212 to $65,162. Such gentrification (many with ONE DC prefer the term displacement) is not unique to this one community. The District, including several long-time distressed neighborhoods, has generally become whiter and wealthier. But Shaw is one where local residents have organized in efforts to assure that they benefit from and are not displaced by development activities.

By engaging in what ONE DC refers to as "participatory democracy," this membership-led organization is confronting several powerful private and public entities to protect residents' interests. Its strategy, as stated on the organization's web page, is one where "people within movements for social change, those directly affected by the issues make the decisions related to the campaign or movement; [they] minimize hierarchy within their organization to maximize shared power and equity of voice; and [they] utilize direct action as an effective means to compel decision-makers to implement decisions made by the community."

The overarching goal is not simply reform but institutional change and social transformation. This is not some vague call to arms. There are specific objectives including, again from the web page, "human rights to affordable housing, living wage jobs, and equitable development." Four recent campaigns are illustrative.

As a precursor of things to come, in 2004, ONE DC organized Kelsey Gardens tenants in fifty-four units (at 7th and P) who were about to be displaced by a church planning to redevelop the property it owned, usurping the residents' first right to purchase their property. Tenants were educated about their rights to purchase their homes and, with legal assistance from Bread for the City and the law firm of Hogan and Hartson, won the rights to affordable housing at the same location for the next fifty years, a $250,000 cash settlement distributed among the tenants, and $10,000 each for relocation costs.

Foreshadowing the Occupy Wall Street movement, in 2010 ONE DC and other supportive civic groups built a tent city and occupied a development site (Parcel 42, 7th and Rhode Island Ave.) in protest of the District's refusal to implement an affordable housing plan that had been part of a previous agreement. For two months, more than 200 residents camped out in the tents. In response, Councilmember

Michael Brown, who serves as the chair of the committee on housing and workforce development, where he is keenly focused on job readiness and housing opportunities for DC residents, visited the encampment at tent city. Brown met with ONE DC and then proposed the "Increase in Housing Affordability Act of 2011." The legislation would set up a funding structure bringing government supported affordable housing projects more in line with the district's needs by setting goals based on median income levels of district residents ($60,902 in 2010) rather than the much higher median for the metropolitan area ($106,100) which has been used previously. The end result would create more affordable housing for more low-income residents of Washington, DC.

Specifically, the bill requires that for all funds the district allocates for affordable housing development:

- Not less than 40 percent shall be allocated to households at or below 30 percent of the district's median income;
- Not less than 80 percent of funds shall be allocated to households at or below 50 percent of the district's median income; and,
- All funds shall be allocated to households at or below 80 percent of the district's median income.

This will not solve the district's affordable housing problem but it would be an important step in the right direction.

In conjunction with the labor organization UNITE HERE, the transgender rights group DC Trans Coalition, and other supporters, ONE DC is recruiting and training neighborhood residents for 500 jobs with the Marriott Marquis Hotel project (currently under construction on the site of the former Convention Center at 9th and Massachusetts Avenue). As required by the New Convention Center Hotel Omnibus Financing and Development Act of 2006, qualified DC residents will be given first consideration for these jobs. ONE DC is working with many area residents who are seeking jobs, several of whom are often difficult to place including ex-offenders and former substance abusers, in efforts to bring jobs and economic opportunities to communities most in need.

Perhaps its most significant victory was the community benefits agreement ONE DC signed with two local developers (Ellis Enterprises and Four Points) for the redevelopment of Progression Place at 7th and S. In return for the community group's support for the project with the DC government, the developers made several commitments. They agreed to set aside twenty housing units for families with incomes below 50 percent of the area median income, and thirty-one of the housing units for families with incomes between 50 percent and 81 percent of the area median income. They agreed to set aside 2,000 square feet of retail space to be made available at below market rates for five years. Hiring goals call for 51 percent of new hires to be DC residents. So far sixty-two jobs have been created with forty-five going to DC residents including seventeen to residents of DC public housing complexes. And a $750,000 community benefits fund was created for investments to be made for services to be determined by area residents. Initially these funds are earmarked for a range of community-based initiatives that include Shaw youth after school programs and support for Shaw-based tenant organizations.

Community advocacy groups in several cities across the country—including New Haven, Pittsburgh, Denver, San Diego, Los Angeles, San Francisco, Seattle, and many others—are using the community benefits model to negotiate developments that facilitate meeting the triple bottom line. ONE DC and Washington DC are hardly alone.

None of this comes easy. Even with the set-asides ONE DC has negotiated, housing affordability persists as a major impediment for working families who would like to live in the District. ONE DC faces challenges in recruiting and training workers for the jobs at the Marriott. And the absence of legally binding requirements in the community benefits agreement has made it more difficult to achieve all the objectives. But ONE DC and its supporters are beginning to change the way developers, city officials, and residents understand and practice community development in the nation's capital.

As noted in its mission statement, "ONE DC has distinguished itself as one of a few organizations in Washington, DC, that moves beyond service provision to build sustainable community capacity and leadership so that low-income people of color can speak for themselves. ONE DC promotes leadership that does not tell others what to do but helps them take charge to build their abilities and skills."

To illustrate, ONE DC has created the Black Workers Center which is a member-led space that builds racial and economic justice through popular education, direct action, and worker-owned businesses. ONE DC raised $1.2 million to purchase a community-controlled building now utilized by several progressive groups including Empower DC, LiUna, the Working Families Party, and Justice First, along with tenants and worker rights organizations. Among its many victories, ONE DC assisted tenants from Mt. Vernon Plaza in their successful campaign to win refunds for two years of rent overpayment from their landlord. HUD Secretary Ben Carson rescinded a proposed regressive rent increase for public housing residents after ONE DC, along with the Right to the City and other local and national organizations, delivered 100,000 signatures protesting this move.

Equitable development may not be the norm in the nation's capital, as illustrated by the multi-million-dollar incentive offered to Amazon in hopes of capturing the second headquarters the company is planning to build. But issues of racial and economic justice are clearly a more explicit concern in development policy and practice, in no small part due to the organizing initiatives of ONE DC and its community partners.

PULLING DEFEAT FROM VICTORY IN THE FIGHT TO BLOCK THE Q STADIUM IN CLEVELAND
By Randy Cunningham

It has taken decades for Cleveland, Ohio, to shake its reputation as the "mistake on the lake." But starting with the 2016 Republican National Convention, a new narrative has taken hold that Cleveland is back and is full of shining promise.

There has been a renaissance of sorts. The downtown is booming with entertainment districts, shining new hotels and convention centers, and upscale housing for the young, hip, and affluent. There are also enclave neighborhoods around University Circle. They have finally succeeded after decades of effort in gentrifying these areas, which now host hip brew pubs, restaurants, and housing.

But the bad old days have not gone away. During the 2008 and 2012 elections, I worked for Barack Obama, canvassing neighborhoods that I was familiar with from my days working for neighborhood-based non-profit housing corporations. I was joined by many of my peers and we had the same response to what we saw. "My God, I thought things were bad in the 1980s when we were working the neighborhoods. Hell, those were the good old days. Things have really gone to hell since then."

Add to this the continuing misbehavior of the Cleveland police as seen in the 2012 maniacal police chase that led to the firing of 137 bullets into the car of two unarmed residents who police thought had fired at them, when the pops were from the car backfiring. Add to this the infamous police shooting death of 12-year-old Tamir Rice in 2014. Add to this continuing decay of those neighborhoods not favored by the wheelers and dealers. Add to this the scandalous rate of lead poisonings among neighborhood children. Add to this the daily body counts from shooting deaths from a state of participatory mayhem in many neighborhoods that defies reason or logic. Compare the breathless boosterism of downtown and favored neighborhoods with these realities and you can understand the rise of a rebellion in Cleveland against a business as usual that has prevailed since the demise of the Kucinich administration in 1979.

The deal to renovate the Quicken Loans Arena (the Q) that houses the Cavaliers, Cleveland's professional basketball team, was announced during the Christmas season so that no one would notice. But the Greater Cleveland Congregations (GCC), an affiliate of Saul Alinsky's Industrial Areas Foundation, the Cuyahoga County Progressive Caucus (which began as the local Bernie Sanders campaign), SEIU 1199, and the Amalgamated Transit Union in Cleveland took notice and began to organize.

The deal arrived at behind closed doors by the city, county, a tourist agency called Destination Cleveland, Quicken Loans billionaire Dan Gilbert, and the Cavaliers' organization was a complex sandwich of agreements to reassign existing taxes generated by the Q with new bond issues for the $160 million public share of the deal. The goal was to add new commercial and entertainment space as part of an atrium that would be added to the existing Q arena. The backers of the deal declared that the renovation was essential to make the Q competitive with other cities for sports, convention, and entertainment events—that without these renovations it was an open question if the Cavs would remain in Cleveland after the end of their 2027 lease. And if they did not remain, then the very existence of civilization in Cuyahoga County was in danger. The bottom line was that the taxpayers of the city and county would once again be shoveling more subsidies down the gullet of a billionaire team owner, with the knowledge that team owners for the Cleveland Browns and Cleveland Indians would be standing in line for more subsidies to keep them happy.

This feast at the public trough followed decades of downtown-oriented tax increases for the public, and property tax abatements and bond issues to subsidize rich developers. This was on top of the fact that city hating state legislators had been cutting public funding for the cities of Ohio for a generation, and that with the election of President Donald Trump, cities would once again be in the bull's eye for cutbacks and austerity. Money could never be found for the social needs of populations such as Cleveland's, but was always available for developers such as Dan Gilbert.

The Cuyahoga County Council was the first body to consider the deal. The public hearings saw standing room only crowds composed of "suits," opponents of the measure, and representatives of the building trades supporting the renovation. The details of the deal were explained in numbers that would put an amphetamine addict to sleep. Always present in the testimony of the backers were two drum beats—jobs, jobs, jobs—and the future of civilized life in the county. The backers drowned the public in numbers and fear.

The opponents, led by the Greater Cleveland Congregations and its allies, spoke of the realities of life in Cleveland's neighborhoods and the unjustness of subsidizing rich developers amid so much unmet need. The Cuyahoga County Progressive Caucus opposed the deal flat out. The Greater Cleveland Congregations was more diplomatic and advocated a dollar-for-dollar match between what was given to the arena, and what would be put in a Community Benefits Fund to help meet community needs such as mental health facilities. They even gave examples of other cities that had made such deals with community organizations as part of stadium and arena deals. The position of the backers of the Q renovation was that a deal was a deal and could not be altered, and that the Cavs employed residents and was generous in its charitable donations.

When the vote came down on the county council, one Democrat and two Republicans opposed the measure.

The action on the Q next moved to the Cleveland City Council. There was a nucleus of opposition from six council people who called themselves the Gateway Six, after the complex that the Q was a part of. In committee, they brought up the consistent theme of the opposition to the project—the jarring visuals of a shining and prosperous downtown, smack up against neighborhoods just a few blocks away that were beset by poverty, despair, and violence. How could the council countenance subsidies for a billionaire team owner in the face of so much want?

The proposal was brought before the council and then withdrawn when the administration saw that the Gateway Six were hanging tough. The second time that the council met on the legislation the backers began the day with a dog-and-pony show proposing a Community Benefits agreement that was laughable in its content. The Cavaliers would refurbish the basketball courts of city schools and recreation centers. They would also direct the ticket receipts that usually were donated by them to charity to Habitat for Humanity to build 100 houses a year in Cleveland. It was nowhere near other Community

Benefits agreements in cities such as Atlanta and Baltimore where the agreements had some real money behind them and had brought real benefits to the cities' neighborhoods. Their show also featured African-American construction workers holding banners touting the jobs, jobs, jobs theme of the proponents.

The proponents peeled off one of the Gateway Six who would vote for the project—Brian Cummins, a former Green Party council member. When he voted, Cummins looked like he would have preferred to be any other place on earth. He did not look up from his desk, and with a barely audible "Yes", consigned himself to infamy. The audience in the council chambers was composed of building trades representatives, Cuyahoga County Progressive Caucus members in their black and blue t-shirts, Greater Cleveland Congregations members in their yellow shirts, and SEIU veterans of the Raise Up $15 campaign raucous in their red shirts. The red shirted SEIU members got up first and marched out of the council chambers to the chant of "Hey, hey, ho, ho, corporate greed has got to go!" The rest of us got up in batches and left the council chambers to gather outside in the hallway to ask the question, "What now?"

Most of us thought it was over with. But word went out that the next night there would be an opposition meeting at the Olivet Institutional Baptist Church on Cleveland's East Side, one of the leading churches in the GCC and one of the most famous African-American churches in the city. Reverend Jawanza Colvin, a speaker in the grand tradition of African-American preaching, said, "No retreat and no surrender." We were going to launch a referendum to put the deal on the ballot starting the next day.

There were a couple of points we had in mind in persisting with the referendum. First was to keep the issue as a political hand grenade that candidates in the November council elections would have to think about. Second was to force the city, county, and Dan Gilbert to the negotiating table. The pittance that was offered before the crucial council vote was arrived at behind closed doors, and with no one else in the room but the backers of the deal. The dominant view in the opposition was that it was an insult, and we were holding out for much more. And we would continue to raise hell until we got it.

The organizers were feeling their way on this, and the first day of petitioning was a trial run. We were run off from a supermarket parking lot but not before we made a good start on gathering signatures. People were not happy with the deal and were willing to sign. I even got a signature from a young man who was fully decked out in Cavaliers regalia. If we could get the volunteers out, we could get the needed signatures by the end of the thirty-day period we were working against.

The campaign began to find its rhythm in the week after signature-gathering began. GCC continued to be the headquarters for turning in signature books, and monitoring how the overall campaign was going, but it began to delegate the actual grunt work of getting signatures to its coalition partners and other sympathizers. The Cuyahoga County Progressive Caucus organized the effort on the West Side of Cleveland, along with its East Side center. A transportation equity group that works on issues of public transit began to gather signatures at transit stops throughout the city, and SEIU hit public "hot spots" downtown. My wife and I started "humping the hood" as we call it, in our ward on the West Side.

Door knocking is hard work as anybody who has done it knows. Most of the time no one is home, so it is low grade ore. We had walk lists of registered voters so there was a high probability of getting good signatures. While the East Side was looked upon as the richest area to gather signatures in, we found a lot of sympathy for the effort in our classic West Side neighborhood (white, blue collar working class) as well. If we could talk to someone, in most cases we would walk away with a signature. What had slipped the attention of so many of the city leaders as they busied themselves in creating Destination Cleveland was the level of antipathy for the Q deal in the forgotten neighborhoods of Cleveland. If Cavaliers' owner Dan Gilbert and Mayor Frank Jackson had "humped the hoods" they would have gotten an earful.

Not that they were deaf and dumb to our work. The mayor began his re-election campaign early with the announcement of a $65 million program for development and services in the neighborhoods just to prove that he had not forgotten the neighborhoods. The Cavaliers began an advertising blitz that boasted of their charitable work in the neighborhoods and attempted to show that they were not just greedy millionaire players and billionaire owners, but were concerned about the rank and file residents of Cleveland as well. There was an even more powerful sign than these PR blitzes that the backers of the Q were getting nervous. Destination Cleveland, the supervising entity for the Q project, put on hold the issuing of bonds for the renovation of the Q until it could see if we succeeded in getting the referendum on the ballot.

We did not just get the 6,000 signatures we needed. We got 20,600 signatures in twenty days in a major bust ass canvassing operation. But the status quo was not going to roll over. After a press conference in front of City Hall, we carried the boxes of signatures up to the office of the Clerk of the City Council, where the acting clerk refused to accept the signatures because the legislation had already passed the City Council and was signed by the Mayor. The opinion of the clerk—who is not an attorney—was that as a result a contract had been made and to accept the signatures would be a violation of the Ohio Constitution. This caused a major confrontation at the Clerk's office where the two leading ministers for GCC presented their hands and said, "Then you are going to have to arrest us." Several of the council who had opposed the Q renovation appeared and had a heated discussion with the Kevin Kelley—the President of Council—

asking him to justify it. He finally agreed to store the boxes at council, but made it clear that this did not mean the signatures were being officially accepted. The council members told the assembled crowd to get legal counsel and sue the city.

The city had its own twist with the goal of pitching the entire question before yet another Republican dominated institution—the Ohio Supreme Court. The City of Cleveland sued itself to get an opinion from the court on the legality of the signatures. Q opponents were represented by a law firm that is famous for its civil rights and liberties work, and the law firm appealed to the court for standing to be involved in the court proceedings. That permission was granted the second week of July.

The result was a stalemate. The county was not selling any bonds until the matter was resolved. An entire construction season was passing away, and all sides were waiting to see what would come out of Columbus. Meanwhile, the jockeying for the fall council and mayoral elections began, and looming over all the races was the question of the Q.

Just because there was a semi-official stalemate did not mean the activists of the campaign were sitting on their hands. Mayor Frank Jackson announced a fundraiser in the rich suburb of Gates Mill, Ohio, at the mansion of insurance tycoon Umberto Fedeli—a reliable contributor to Republican candidates and causes.

We scouted out the site and after some debate, visited the village hall of Gates Mill to let the police chief know what was coming. The police chief was very solicitous and said we could have an area across from the mansion for our rally.

Amid a crazed pitch of activist creativity, we came up with a name for the event—Frank's Fat Cat Festival. The word went out, and we started collecting buy-ins from SEIU 1199, the new Democratic Socialists of America chapter, along with several other groups. There are more convenient places to have a demonstration than this subdivision in Gates Mill. This was a major worry of ours that we solved by arranging a shuttle from a nearby Metroparks parking lot to the site. Another problem was the site required a significant drive from Cleveland and good GPS to find.

About ten of us gathered at the site and we started to grouse to one another that this was going to be a "wear a paper sack over your head" moment, when we started hearing the percussion section of the Raise Up Cleveland activists of SEIU. Around the corner came the red shirts and bull-horns that announced that the party had begun.

By now, we had a crowd of forty that sounded like a hundred, and the guests began to arrive in Mercedes, top of the line luxury SUV's, a few Maseratis, and other high-end vehicles. We went around pasting play money on people's shirts. The Raise Up Cleveland group started yelling "Meow!!" at the fat cat guests. We began to get bored with the old "hey, hey, ho, ho" chants. I came up with one that even caused the cops to laugh, "No hors d'oeuvres! No peace!!!" Umberto Fedeli did bring out a pizza for the demonstrators, who responded by telling him, "No pizza. We want Frank."

We got good coverage, but unfortunately there was some collateral damage suffered by the Greater Cleveland Congregations for the action. Four of their member congregations—two churches and two Jewish temples—withdrew from the coalition, charging that it had become political and had adopted tactics that were too militant. GCC declared that while they regretted the departure of their former coalition members, the departure was not going to cause them to waver on the Q or on their broader mission of social justice.

The waiting game on the Ohio Supreme Court finally ended on August 11 when the court in a 4-3 decision ordered the Cleveland City Council Clerk to begin the signature count. Then on August 28, Dan Gilbert owner of the Cavaliers, threw in the towel and pulled out of the deal. We were handed one of the greatest victories we have ever had. Or so we thought.

On August 31 it was announced that the Greater Cleveland Congregations, without consulting with or even informing the other coalition members, had made an agreement with County Administrator Armond Budish for two mental health clinics to be built—one on the West Side of Cleveland and one on the East Side. The agreement was very general and Budish wrote in a letter saying that it depended on county finances and what he called "best practices" for providing mental health and drug addiction treatment. One could read the terms of the agreement repeatedly and still have questions about just what it was that was agreed to, and what were the guarantees that promises would be kept.

It was nowhere close to the original proposal for a community benefits agreement and left the original Q deal intact. There were no guarantees because GCC's part of the bargain was to withdraw the petition for the referendum, which was the club the campaign was holding over the heads of the city, county, and the Cavaliers franchise. GCC members made up the petition committee. Legally they could do it. They withdrew the petition. There would be no referendum and the campaign was dead.

The Greater Cleveland Congregations faced a hurricane of recrimination from the city establishment after Gilbert dropped out of the deal. It paled before the fury that hit them from their coalition partners. The words "betrayal", "traitors", and "sell-outs" were some of the more charitable accusations that were hurled at them. What infuriated the activists from all the groups was that after eight months of organizing, and after all the work that went into collecting 20,600 signatures in under thirty days, it was all thrown away for the most minimal of benefits.

For the backers of the Q deal, the caving of the GCC was a miracle, and work began immediately to get the project back on track after months of delays because of the opposition. That the Q project was alive and well was confirmed on September 6, when it was announced that the Cavaliers were back as partners and it was full speed ahead with the project. This turn of events made me suspect that Dan Gilbert's withdrawal from the deal was a ruse. Social media in Cleveland worked overtime speculating about what really happened behind the scenes, and all manner of lurid schemes and conspiracies were entertained.

So, what can we say now? First, the activist community in Cleveland that invested its heart and soul into this epic battle was in shock and many of us were frankly depressed in the aftermath of GCC's action. Second, the Greater Cleveland Congregations has become a pariah and a generation of Cleveland activists will never again trust them or work with them. They have yet to realize or admit to just how much they have lost for what they call a win. Third, to end on a positive note we should give ourselves credit for almost pulling off one of the greatest popular victories seen in Cleveland since the campaign to save Muni Light during the Kucinich administration. An editorial on September 3, 2017, in Crain's Cleveland Business—hardly a friend of our coalition—noticed the importance of what we did:".....but if there's one lesson we've learned, it's that the same sort of deals that worked twenty-five years ago won't work in the Cleveland of today."

We changed the city. We will be back.

ROAD BLOCK: Fighting the Freeway in Little Rock
By Darcy Pumphrey

Urban interstate construction in the 20th century immensely affected the patterns of daily life in cities across the United States. City and highway planners as well as government officials saw urban interstates as a way to solve urban issues of the 20th century through the redevelopment of the central business district, the removal of slums, and the improvement of access to downtown. However, the effects of urban interstates were often quite different from the original intentions: they altered transportation patterns to rely less on public transportation, they moved economic activity away from a centralized downtown, they disrupted neighborhoods and business districts, they caused prominent divisions in cities along racial and economic lines, and they caused the rapid expansion of cities into suburbs.

Interstate 630 (I-630), a 7.4-mile stretch of roadway bisecting Little Rock, Arkansas, started in 1958 with the acquisition of right-of-way. The project experienced delays from financial issues as well as legal action brought on by an active group of citizens that worked to slow the freeway's encroachment on and division of Little Rock. The most prominent and outspoken organization fighting the I-630 project was Arkansas Community Organizations for Reform Now (ACORN), a community organization founded by Wade Rathke in 1970. ACORN served as the catalyst for the Little Rock freeway resistance movement's grassroots organization and neighborhood activism and largely led the fight to stop I-630. Despite ACORN's efforts, crews finally completed construction on I-630 in 1985, significantly altering transportation patterns, neighborhood demographics, and locations of economic centers. Nevertheless, the freeway resistance movement in Little Rock did gain influence over many key decisions within the planning and construction process.

The construction of I-630 spanned two distinct periods of freeway resistance. During the 1950s and early 1960s, freeway planners built roads with limited opposition and many citizens welcomed the routes through their cities as a sign of progress. As a result of this mindset, highway departments completed many freeway projects that began during this time with minimal resistance from the community. This was the case in Little Rock, where the main difficulty during those early years of freeway route planning and construction involved securing the funding to carry out the project.

However, as the 1970s approached, many citizens began to feel the impact of these large-scale road projects and questioned the need for the resulting damage to the fabric of their cities and neighborhoods. At the same time, the federal government enacted laws such as the National Environmental Policy Act (NEPA), which gave freeway opposition groups legal ground to fight urban interstate projects. The freeway resistance movement in Little Rock began to coalesce and gain legitimacy during the early 1970s with the establishment of ACORN. The Arkansas Highway and Transportation Department soon realized that funding issues were no longer the only obstacle for the I-630 project. This change would draw out construction of the nearly eight-mile interstate for more than 25 years.

The proposed route connected Interstate 430 (I-430) in the western and more underdeveloped part of the city with Interstate 30 (I-30) toward the eastern edge of downtown Little Rock. Notably intrusive was the section from Park Street east to I-30 that cut through downtown Little Rock's well-established neighborhoods, like the MacArthur Park Historic District, and business districts, like the Ninth Street African-American business district. The route also narrowly missed such landmarks and institutions as Mount Holly Cemetery, Arkansas Children's Hospital, the Arkansas State Capitol, Philander Smith College, and MacArthur Park. This downtown section proved to be the most controversial and time-consuming segment of the proposed project.

During the 1960s, the proposed route, then referred to as the East-West Expressway, was not part of the federal interstate highway system. It was a project of the city of Little Rock and the Arkansas highway department. They managed to clear some of the right-of-way and constructed a mile section of the route by 1969; however, they struggled to find ways to continue funding this massive undertaking. In March 1970, highway department Director Ward Goodman wrote to Frank C. Turner, administrator for the Federal Highway Administration, formally requesting the addition of the East-West Expressway in the interstate highway system. Inclusion in the system meant the federal government would fund construction of the route at 90 percent. The state government would be responsible for the remaining 10 percent, while the city would be relieved of further financial obligations.

Wilbur D. Mills of Kensett, Arkansas, the influential United States Representative and head of the powerful Ways and Means Committee, took special interest in the project and discussed it with Turner. Representative Mills' spokesman noted that the he was hopeful about an approval of the request. However, the Bureau of Public

Roads initially denied the inclusion of the route in the interstate system. Rex C. Leathers, Little Rock division engineer for the bureau, stated that, "All mileage had been allocated and none is available for the addition or extension of routes," but the request was "being held for future consideration if and when mileage becomes available." Shortly thereafter, in June 1970, the federal government informed Representative Mills of the plans to add the route although they did not allow the congressman to make an official announcement until after the November general elections. As a result, the route also received a new name: Interstate 630.

Shortly after Representative Mills' announcement of the route's inclusion, the Little Rock City Board adopted a resolution on December 21 designating the expressway as the Wilbur D. Mills Freeway in recognition of the congressman's efforts to get the route included in the Interstate Highway System. The Arkansas Highway Commission (AHC) determined that the Federal Manual on Uniform Traffic Control Devices prohibits the renaming of numbered highways after persons. While the city could unofficially refer to the route as the Wilbur D. Mills Freeway, it was officially known as Interstate 630.

The construction of I-630 started to move forward quickly once the route was included in the Interstate Highway System. But with federal funding came federal rules and regulations with which the AHC had to adhere. Most notably, the National Environmental Policy Act (NEPA) of 1969 required the completion of an Environmental Impact Statement (EIS) detailing the environmental consequences of any project receiving federal funding. Although the city and state had already purchased, cleared, and constructed some of the route (including a one-mile segment from Pine Street east to Dennison Street that opened on April 22, 1969, and citizens often referred to in jest as the "World's Shortest Freeway") prior to federal funding, the I-630 project was not exempt from these federal requirements.

The Arkansas highways department released its original draft environmental impact statement for the I-630 project in February 1972. The statement's main purpose was to examine the environmental impact of the federally funded project and recommend ways to mitigate potential negative impacts on the affected area. The highways department held a public hearing on the design, as required for the environmental impact statement review, on March 14, 1972. Views among the hearing's 350 to 400 participants ranged from full support, to apprehensive acceptance, to complete disapproval of the project. Don R. Venhaus, director of Little Rock's Department of Community Development, said that I-630 would "become the most significant traffic transportation artery in this community the day it is opened for traffic from I-430 to I-30." Little Rock citizen and director of the Arkansas Consumer Center, Fred Cowan, spoke about the issue of increased racial segregation as a result of the interstate. Cowan questioned the placement of an interstate through the heart of Little Rock, expressing concern that the route leading out to the suburbs would "encourage even more segregation of housing as it has in other cities."

The group that would eventually be the most outspoken in opposition to the I-630 project, ACORN, released a response to the proposal for I-630 in December 1972 noting their opposition to "the continuation of the Interstate 630 project since the AHTD has never sincerely considered the justified aspirations of residents living in those neighborhoods which are tentatively planned to be partially extinguished. Until such inconsideration and inconsistencies within the EIS are changed from rhetoric to guaranteed action, ACORN asks that all construction be discontinued immediately." This response was the first of many critiques of the interstate project ACORN leveled at the highways department over the next few years.

ACORN felt that the highway department's environmental impact statement simply justified the I-630 project and failed to impartially consider environmental and societal implications of the interstate on the surrounding areas. Some of the organization's specific concerns included the environmental impact statement's use of language assuming the inevitability of the project's completion, and the diversion of funds from other projects—designed to improve sometimes dangerous and inadequate state routes—in order to construct I-630 which would allow commuters "to arrive at their destination three minutes faster." The group also argued that I-630 would not serve interstate travelers but would more closely resemble an "urban commuterway" and therefore should not be part of the interstate highway system. Finally, ACORN expressed concern that the interstate "will...constitute a physical barrier between black and white neighborhoods," and that relocation efforts offered a limited number of housing options for displaced citizens. If the highways department did not guarantee adequate mitigation efforts for these public concerns then ACORN insisted that the project "be suspended and funds withdrawn."

ACORN began to consider legal action to stop the project and felt that they had a strong case against the highway department and their environmental impact statement. In response to what it felt was a "grossly inadequate" environmental impact statement, the organization set up the ACORN Neighborhood Legal Defense Fund in August 1973 to raise money for legal action against the highway department as part of the community organization's "continuing effort to insure minimal disruption to Little Rock neighborhoods." ACORN raised enough funds to file a lawsuit against federal and state highway officials on November 9, 1973. Little Rock attorney Jack Lavey provided his services to the plaintiffs *pro bono*.

With the lawsuit in place, divisions among community members and organizations became clearer as those against the interstate aligned behind ACORN and those in support of the project intervened in the lawsuit on behalf of the state and federal governments. In July 1974 the city of Little Rock joined the lawsuit in support of the defendants. The city had already spent over $3 million on the

completed section of the interstate from Rice Street to University Avenue and did not want to see this section "rendered virtually useless" through an early termination of the project. The city expressed concern about high traffic volumes and congestion that they felt would result without the presence of a complete interstate and noted the presence of extensive development and rezoning along the proposed route completed in anticipation of the interstate.

The Little Rock School District and the Baptist Medical Center also intervened in the lawsuit on the state and federal governments' behalf. The highways department had agreed to fund a new elementary school for the school district to replace the aging Parham Elementary School located in the right-of-way of the interchange between I-630 and I-30. The Baptist Medical Center intervened in the lawsuit because they had selected a location for their newly constructed medical facility along the western end of the planned I-630 route with the idea that a completed I-630 would provide easy access to their medical facilities. With the court battle looming, the I-630 project appeared to have many supporters.

The case went to trial September 16, 1974, under federal Judge J. Smith Henley. ACORN brought in a number of witnesses to testify on the inadequacy of the environmental impact statement including Dr. James B. Sullivan, an air-quality expert from Washington, DC, who testified that it was "technically...terrible" and included claims about air pollution that were "unsubstantiated by air quality tests." Dr. Malcolm Getz, a Vanderbilt University economics professor, argued that the environmental impact statement needed to examine whether or not a quicker commute downtown was worth depressing the land values within one-quarter mile along the route. A consultant on transportation planning and policy based in Berkeley, California, Robert A. Burco, testified that the highway department did not consider alternatives and did not consider any public objections within its environmental impact statement. During Burco's testimony he emphasized, "There are alternatives. They simply have not been addressed" or "seriously considered."

Testifying on behalf of the defense, Jason Rouby, the director of the central Arkansas planning organization Metroplan, stressed that downtown Little Rock would "deteriorate further" without the construction of I-630 as businesses would move toward the suburbs and western Little Rock. Rouby viewed I-630 as a way to provide easier access to downtown businesses and did not see the interstate as a substantial barrier to neighborhoods.

The highway department continued construction on the freeway throughout the September 1974 trial and during the time between the trial's conclusion and when Judge Henley issued his ruling on the case. Ten months after the court proceedings, on July 28, 1975, Judge Henley ruled that the environmental impact statement was inadequate and did not sufficiently consider design alternatives. The department would have to create a new environmental impact statement and during the interim they would have to suspend some of their construction on I-630 mainly in the downtown section from Dennison Street east to I-30. However, Judge Henley permitted the department to continue to acquire right-of-way properties in the downtown section with the caveat that they could only purchase properties through voluntary sales and not through condemnation. Judge Henley also allowed construction to continue along the less densely populated route from University Avenue west to I-430 citing "the need for rapid access to the new [Baptist] Medical Center."

ACORN viewed Judge Henley's decision as a success because it required the department to hold new public hearings to review a newly-created environmental impact statement. The Chief Organizer of ACORN, Wade Rathke, explained that these public hearings offered the opportunity to "open up very serious consideration at every step of the process where there may be fights engaged... to make this thing right."

Almost two years after Judge Henley's ruling, the Arkansas highway department issued their first draft of the second environmental impact statement in April 1977. In the second impact statement, the department greatly expanded the section on possible alternatives to the planned I-630 construction, from ten paragraphs to twenty-nine pages. Among the alternatives considered, the highway department examined the possibility of moving the eastern section of the route north or south of the existing design, but they determined that "because of the partially completed status of the project...the route already selected would result in the fewest adverse effects."

The department also considered placing the section of the route running alongside MacArthur Park in a tunnel due to the historical significance of the area and surrounding buildings, but they determined this option to be "economically unfeasible." The second statement came to the same conclusion as the original—that the route already chosen was the best option for an east-west freeway in Little Rock. Over the next year, the draft of the second statement went through several public hearings as required by law. The highways department submitted the final draft of the second environmental impact statement on July 14, 1978, and asked to have the injunction on construction removed.

ACORN asserted that the second statement was also inadequate. Some of ACORN's main issues with the second statement included concerns that the report did not consider a "no-build alternative," did not examine the alternatives of building four lanes as opposed to six lanes, did not "reasonably and objectively analyze and evaluate the mass transit alternative," and did not consider the freeway's socio-economic impact on minorities.

Judge G. Thomas Eisele presided over the hearing on the second environmental impact statement during the week of October 30, 1978. ACORN presented two witnesses during the hearing. The first was Dr. Fred Johnson, an associate professor of economics at the University of Alabama, who felt that the second environmental impact statement did not "analyze whether the cost justified the benefits of the proposed route or alternatives" as required by the federal highway planning manuals. The second witness was Jack Smyth, a consulting engineer and urban planner from Aston, Pennsylvania, who criticized the second statement on several points. He accused the highway department of using "grossly overblown" projected traffic volumes on which to base the need for completion of the project; creating a road design with too many hazards such as the placement of numerous ramps within a short distance; and not adequately exploring the costs of "meaningful alternatives."

Witnesses for the defendants argued in support of the second environmental impact statement and the proposed design by refuting many of Smyth's arguments against the freeway route and statement's data. Defense witness Sanford M. Wilbourn, president of Garver & Garver, Inc., spoke to the inevitability of the planned freeway design noting, "You've already cut a swath through Little Rock and relocated 90 percent [of the occupants in the right-of-way]." Starting a completely new route for the remaining section of the freeway instead of using the area already cleared, he argued, was ridiculous and would cause even more environmental damage.

The five-day hearing ended on October 3, 1978, and Judge Eisele stated that he would decide on the second environmental impact statement as soon as possible. About six months later, on April 27, 1979, Judge Eisele announced the dismissal of the lawsuit, ruling that the second environmental impact statement met all of the requirements of federal laws and regulations. His thirty-page opinion, released on May 7, 1979, called the data used by the highways department "sufficiently accurate" and insisted, "no such error [had] been shown to undermine the methodology used or the essential reliability of the data." At this point ACORN had exhausted their legal options and the I-630 project moved forward. The highway department prepared to quickly open bids on the eastern section of the project and a completed I-630 finally opened on September 30, 1985, more than twenty-five years after the project began.

The ultimate downfall of ACORN's litigation can be traced to their failure to gain the support of influential community leaders and the timing of their lawsuit. Unfortunately for the Little Rock freeway resistance movement, area politicians were largely pro-freeway, including influential U.S. Representative Wilbur D. Mills and several sitting and former mayors of Little Rock who felt that I-630 would modernize the city and minimize traffic congestion. Even public figures who expressed hesitancy about the construction of I-630 still desired its completion. State Representative Robert Johnston and Little Rock School Board member Herb Rule questioned the project's effect on the community and requested better mitigation measures, but this was not the strong or widespread backing that ACORN needed to advance their fight.

Much of the business community was also supportive of the route. Many businessmen touted the project's potential to invigorate the city's central business district like Little Rock Chamber of Commerce President Werner C. Knoop, who emphasized that the completion of the route was "probably the single most important project pending to assure the continued rebuilding of the downtown area." ACORN also felt that they came up short with support from prominent journalists and newspapers as well, noting that they "were unable to swing to [ACORN's] position the city's major newspaper [the *Arkansas Gazette*] which had previously supported similar citizens campaigns in other cities, that is, saving Overton Park in Memphis from the path of an expressway."

Yet for all of ACORN's work against the freeway, which certainly demonstrated persistent neighborhood activism with a strong message and network of citizens, crucially the group's downfall was in their timing. Their efforts came too late to stop the freeway as the city and state had already purchased and cleared a large portion of the right-of-way by the time ACORN first organized as a group in the early 1970s. As an editorial in the *Arkansas Gazette* suggested, "[t]he time for real protest or objection was in the 1950s." Though ACORN acted against the first environmental impact statement and made a strong case, the wide swath of cleared land bisecting the city suggested the inevitability of the project. Even as Judge Henley ruled that the first environmental impact statement was inadequate, he spoke to the certainty of the route noting "the court thinks it fair to say that in all probability an adequate statement will eventually be submitted and approved, and that the project east of Dennison will be built substantially along the route that has been delineated for years."

The battle over I-630 reflected the changes in how citizens responded to highway departments' plans across the nation. Interstate projects started in the 1950s and early 1960s often faced little opposition and, as a result, highway departments completed these routes in a timely manner. With the passage of NEPA in 1969, governmental agencies found their decisions more often challenged by anti-freeway groups with new legal tools to fight interstate plans. Such resistance in Little Rock, which initially caught the highway department by surprise, eventually became the norm. Unfortunately for Little Rock freeway opponents, this nationwide shift came too late to stop I-630, which was an active project even before it became part of the Interstate Highway System in 1970.

The movement in Little Rock did not have the advantage of fighting only proposed drawings and plans; they were fighting a route that was already making a highly visible mark across town. Further complicating their goal was the fact that many businesses anticipated its construction and several citizens had already sold their houses to the highway department and relocated. Such factors made I-630 seem inevitable, an issue that ACORN recognized as a shortcoming in their fight when they reflected in 1977: "The Mills Freeway was almost a reality when ACORN kicked its organizing machine into motion."

While ACORN did not succeed in ultimately stopping the project, it produced a strong grassroots movement that garnered some victories including efforts to mitigate the impact of the project and force the highway department listen to citizens. One way they achieved this was to publicize the adverse impacts they felt the interstate construction would cause, stating that the main goal of their movement "was to clearly establish to public officials what citizens really thought about the project." Tactics included reaching out to the media and the highway department, organizing neighborhood groups, and attacking the environmental impact statement through legal avenues. They also followed the highway department into the affected neighborhoods. In 1974 the highway department set up a mobile office in the neighborhoods along the route's vicinity in order to gather citizens' opinions on the project and listen to their concerns. ACORN saw the mobile office as an effort to "minimize future citizen opposition" against the department and the I-630 project noting that while there were department employees present to listen to the residents "their concerns [went] no further than the van." The organization countered the highway department mobile office by placing an "ACORN Counter Van" nearby in order to share with residents "how to organize to protect their lives from overly ambitious highway planners."

Many smaller organizations emerged from ACORN's membership to fight aspects of the proposed freeway while maintaining an affiliation with the parent organization. The Mills Freeway Neighborhood Committee challenged the Little Rock Planning Commission's zoning and land-use near the route. The Mills Action Coalition (MAC) was instrumental in raising funds to pursue legal action against the Arkansas highway department. Finally, the MacArthur Park Neighborhood Association continued its opposition to the freeway throughout the late 1970s, calling attention to the importance of maintaining the historic aesthetic of their neighborhood and preventing a re-segregation of the community. These affiliate groups, many of which sprouted from the affected neighborhoods, helped create a larger reach for ACORN's campaign.

ACORN prided itself on class cooperation, describing their resistance movement as "somewhat unique because the fight was exclusively orchestrated by low-and moderate-income residents of Little Rock's central city." ACORN noted that other freeway fights often involved "upper or middle-upper income environmental devotees" but "the Mills controversy was clearly a gut issue for ACORN working families who did not wish their neighborhoods destroyed." ACORN's lawsuit, though ultimately unsuccessful, gave these community groups a more prominent voice and had a significant impact on the final outcome of the I-630 project. The litigation placed an injunction on the project from 1975 and 1979, giving opponents time to further examine and question the route and its impact on the city. As a result, multiple mitigation measures were agreed upon between the highway department and the community regarding the depth of the below-grade roadway; specific landscaping details; the types of lighting, signs, fences, and other architectural details in the interstate and right-of-way area; and the elimination of frontage roads and ramps in certain areas.

While ACORN did not stop I-630 from becoming a reality, their efforts slowed construction and allowed citizens to question the design and ultimately minimize the road's impact. Perhaps more significantly, ACORN and the freeway resistance movement helped change the highway department's approach to the planning and the construction of such imposing structures that significantly alter a city's fabric. ACORN reflected in 1977 that, "A real victory had been won, in that ordinary citizens have learned that you can fight institutions like the Highway Department. The AHTD was noticeably shaken up by our challenge and will not be so quick to assume that they can force their highway plans through in the future."

Such successes of the freeway resistance movement, however, are obscured by what many see as the ultimate results of its failure, foreshadowed by ACORN's 1973 response to the first environmental impact statement: "If constructed, this 'Interstate' will be a substantial racial divider, with blacks realistically allotted housing mobility only south of the project from downtown westward to University [Avenue]. More businesses will continue to move westward...To contend that the 'Interstate' will save the city by destroying its physical structure needs logical documentation."

Some scholars and journalists recognized the truth of ACORN's predictions, among them journalists Jay Barth and David Koon in the *Arkansas Times*; Chad Day in the *Arkansas Democrat-Gazette*; and author Jay Jennings. All have suggested that ACORN's predictions—made twelve years before the 1985 completion of I-630—have become Little Rock's reality.

Certainly, Little Rock would be a different city had the freeway resistance movement succeeded in their efforts. Maybe the neighborhoods to the north and south of the route would be more integrated than they are today. Maybe West Little Rock would still be rolling hills and quiet forests. Maybe downtown would be the vibrant center of commerce it was in the first half of the twentieth century. Regardless of how I-630 changed Little Rock, the movement against its construction can offer important lessons for future groups looking to alter the course of a city's development.

PARTICIPATORY PLANNING CAMPAIGN IN LAST DITCH EFFORT TO SAVE MEMPHIS PUBLIC HOUSING
By Kenneth M. Reardon and Antonio Raciti

In the fall of 2010, the Memphis Housing Authority invited leaders of the Vance Avenue neighborhood along with faculty from the University of Memphis graduate program in city and regional planning to join them in preparing a comprehensive revitalization plan for this historic African-American neighborhood. After it committed $250,000 to the project, the housing authority planned to seek matching funds to support this comprehensive planning process from the U.S. Department of Housing and Urban Development (HUD) Choice Neighborhoods Program. Skeptical of the housing authority's newly articulated commitment to participatory planning and cooperative development, local residents and their university allies were initially reluctant to join what they feared might be another example of top-down planning.

However, believing they would have greater influence over the outcome of the planning process as active participants, local leaders ultimately decided to accept the housing authority's invitation asking their University planning colleagues to join them in this process. During the winter of 2010, a small group of resident leaders and university faculty worked with a housing authority consultant to prepare a Choice Neighborhood Planning Grant Application. The grant would support a highly participatory process for creating a comprehensive revitalization plan for this once-vibrant African-American neighborhood where Ida B. Wells, Benjamin L. Hooks, Rufus Thomas, and Mavis Staples once lived and worked.

In March 2011, U.S. Congressman Steve Cohen announced that Memphis had been selected as one of just seventeen cities from an applicant pool of one hundred and nine communities that would be receiving Choice Neighborhood Planning Grants from HUD. During the following year, leaders of the Vance Avenue Collaborative, a coalition of twenty-two neighborhood-based organizations serving the area, with the assistance of university students and faculty, engaged more than 1,000 local residents, business owners, and institutional leaders in a bottom-up planning process that generated widespread interest in and support for the project.

As part of this process, oral histories were gathered from area seniors; past reports, studies, and plans were reviewed; population, employment, and housing trends were analyzed. In addition, community assets were mapped by local stakeholders and neighborhood characteristics were documented by 1,500 resident-generated photographs, and two hundred residents, business owners, and institutional leaders were interviewed regarding their perceptions of existing conditions and future development options. Focus groups were organized involving area youth, business owners, senior citizens, service providers, and religious leaders. Also, land use, building conditions, and infrastructure maintenance conditions were surveyed. The results of these research activities were presented and analyzed at monthly planning meetings which eighty to one hundred local stakeholders regularly attended.

In April 2012, more than one hundred and fifty local stakeholders participated in a day-long Neighborhood Summit to further analyze these findings, establish an overall vision for neighborhood's future development, and brainstorm specific neighborhood improvement projects designed to transform this long-suffering residential community into a desirable neighborhood of choice. After much debate, the assembled stakeholders committed themselves to collaborating with local officials "to transform the Vance Avenue community into the nation's leading example of Dr. Martin Luther King Jr.'s ideal of the beloved community—a place where residents work together to overcome the historic racial and class divisions that have long plagued Memphis and other Southern cities to support individuals, regardless of their socioeconomic status, in reaching their maximum God-given potential."

Following the adoption of this statement as their overall development goal, local stakeholders formulated a comprehensive set of development objectives to improve environmental conditions; enhance public education; re-establish local retail services; insure primary health care access; generate employment and business opportunities; preserve and expand affordable housing options; celebrate the area's extraordinary civil rights history; and strengthen its transportation connections to regional educational, employment, and cultural centers.

During the summer of 2012, more than one hundred neighborhood residents and stakeholders attended a series of issue specific meetings that generated more than thirty-three immediate, short, and long-term revitalization proposals to be carried out as part of the emerging Vance Avenue Community Transformation Plan. Among the most important of the immediate-term projects designed to jump-start the neighborhood revitalization process was the preservation and improvement of Foote Homes—the city's last public housing project located in the heart of the community.

When housing authority officials reviewed the data emerging out of the planning process which indicated that two out of three residents strongly supported the preservation and improvement of this complex which the housing authority had long ago decided to demolish, the agency took quick action! They fired the project's university planners; ended the citizen consultation process; shut down the website used to update interested parties about the plan; and suspended regular meetings of the Vance Avenue Choice Neighborhood Project management and consultant teams.

With all of the historic, demographic, environmental, economic, and social data needed to complete an empirically-based comprehensive plan at hand, the university planners who had staffed the planning process met with leaders of the local organizations which were responsible for the majority of the resident participation in the process to ask if they wanted to see the plan completed. The leaders of all but two of these tenant organizations, neighborhood associations, religious congregations, social service agencies, labor unions, environmental justice groups, and civil rights organizations voiced a

strong desire to see the plan that more than 1,000 of their neighbors had helped create be completed.

With the strong support of these organizations, university students and faculty spent August and September of 2012 working with local leaders to create a preliminary draft of Vance Avenue Community Transformation Plan. This 104-page document articulated a resident-inspired alternative to the city's historic HOPE VI model of area redevelopment. This is an approach in which public housing tenants are involuntarily relocated, existing complexes are demolished, areas are renamed and rebranded, and "mixed income" housing is constructed in which fewer than 15 percent of the former public housing tenants are rehoused.

On September 12, 2012, one hundred and fifty neighborhood residents, area stakeholders, media representatives and local officials crowded into the Saint Patrick Community Center to hear a detailed presentation of the preliminary draft of the Vance Avenue Community Transformation Plan. After more than an hour of spirited questioning and debate, the plan received the overwhelming support of those assembled who also endorsed a Vance Avenue Collaborative proposal to seek city council adoption of the plan. Unbeknownst to those meeting at St. Patrick, the housing authority had earlier that same day applied to the City of Memphis/Shelby County Community Redevelopment Agency to establish a new Downtown Tax Incremental Financing (TIF) district to generate $102 million to cover the local share of their Heritage Trail Plan.

This plan, which had never been presented to the community or their elected representatives, was designed to transform the Vance Avenue neighborhood into a destination tourism district similar to New Orleans' French Quarter, Kansas City's 18th and Vine, and Harlem's 125th Street neighborhoods through the selective celebration of the area's extraordinary civil rights history. As expected, the plan featured the demolition of Foote Homes; the construction of 600-800 units of mixed-income replacement housing; construction of miles of new roads to re-establish the area's former gridded street pattern; improvement of existing playgrounds and parks; the building of several new recreational facilities; creation of a historical walking trail; and the implementation of a major streetscape improvement initiative. The implementation of the housing authority's Heritage Trail Plan under the housing authority's TIF Financing proposal, would absorb 98 percent of the downtown's future property tax increases for the coming twenty years. The establishment of the TIF would also require the Community Redevelopment Agency to declare the target area "blighted" and designate a local redevelopment agency with eminent domain powers to oversee the implementation of the plan's major elements.

In the days following the neighborhood's endorsement of the resident-generated Vance Avenue Community Transformation Plan and the housing authority's submission of their own Heritage Trail TIF-based financing proposal, small delegations of the Vance Avenue Collaborative members began meeting with members of the city council's planning and zoning committee. During the first of these meetings, Council-member Edmund Ford, chair of this important committee, offered to hold a public hearing on the merits of the Vance Avenue Community Transformation Plan in early October. After securing the support of the majority of the councilpersons on this committee, the Vance Avenue Collaborative held a press conference to present the basic outlines of their plan and to describe the grassroots organizing campaign they were launching to secure its adoption by the Memphis City Council.

Seventy-five community residents, area stakeholders, religious leaders, labor officials, environmental activists, and elected officials attended this event at which a broad cross-section of local civic organizations pledged their support for the Vance Avenue Community Transformation Plan. Highlights of this press conference dominated local newspaper and television coverage for days generating numerous offers of support from adjacent neighborhoods, local developers, and county officials.

Several weeks after the press conference, on the day of the council's planning and zoning committee hearing on the plan, fifty neighborhood residents and their allies met at St. Patrick Church for an early morning-prayer service led by Fr. Tim Sullivan. Following the service, participants picked up placards designed in the image of the iconic 1968 sanitation workers strike posters which read "We Are a Community—Improve—Don't Remove Foote Homes" and left the church singing "We Shall Not be Removed". The group—which planned to march along the historic route used by the Sanitation Workers during their daily non violent marches to city hall in 1968—stopped shortly after leaving the church at the nearby Clayborn Temple where Dr. King first pledged his support to this historic labor struggle.

They did so to place a bouquet of flowers and to observe a few minutes of silence in memory of Dr. King who died just blocks away on the balcony of the Lorraine Motel and all those who died in the struggle for civil rights in the South. Following this activity, the marchers made their way to city hall distributing flyers and "Improve Don't Remove" stickers to the large number of noontime patrons crowding the restaurants lining the city's Main Street pedestrian mall. Among the marchers was retired school teacher and long-time civil rights activist Allen Stiles, a member of Saint Patrick's Church. After participating in the city's first downtown lunch counter sit-ins, he had marched with Dr. King in support of the sanitation workers.

When the marchers arrived at city hall, they were joined by dozens of other public housing tenants and neighborhood supporters who crowded into a city council conference room for the planning and zoning committee meeting. Upon entering this room, the marchers were greeted by Robert Lipscomb, long-time executive director of the Memphis Housing Authority and director of the city of Memphis

division of housing and community development, who was appearing before the committee on an unrelated budgetary item. Following his budget presentation, Lipscomb advised the committee against considering our plan which he said, "reflected a divide and conquer strategy used to keep the poor in their place as old as the Bible."

Undeterred by these remarks, four local leaders took turns describing the major elements and expected benefits of the Vance Avenue Community Transformation Plan. Following their remarks, Councilwoman Janis Fullilove, who grew up in Foote Homes, made a motion to endorse the resident-generated plan so it could be forwarded to the full Council for a consideration before advancing to the Memphis/Shelby County land use control board (a.k.a. planning commission) for approval. Following a brief question and answer period, the planning and zoning committee voted 4-0 to endorse the resident-driven plan over the clear opposition of the housing authority's powerful executive director.

In the weeks following this historic city council vote in support of the preservation of Foote Homes, Vance Avenue Collaborative members mobilized residents and stakeholders on three separate occasions to attend meetings of the full city council at which the Vance Avenue Community Transformation Plan was scheduled to be discussed and voted upon. At the beginning of the first two of these city council meetings, the city council president announced that the item had been dropped from the agenda. At the third meeting, the city council president introduced the attorney for the city council, Alan Wade, who made a verbal statement indicating that the Vance Avenue Community Transformation Plan could not be taken up by the city council because it affected an existing urban renewal area under the jurisdiction of the city of Memphis Division of Housing and Community Development. Pressed by Collaborative leaders and their council supporters to produce a written copy of what residents began to quickly refer to as the "immaculate conception" opinion he agreed, under pressure, to do so. In the more than two months that have transpired since this city council hearing, Mr. Wade has been unable to produce this document.

While these events were taking place before the city council in November and December of 2012, the housing authority's staff was quietly seeking the Memphis/Shelby Community Development Agency's support for their $102 million TIF Proposal. At a series of finance committee and general membership meetings held before and after Christmas, housing authority representatives sought to convince this combined city/county board of the benefits of the Heritage Plan and its TIF-based financing proposal. At each of these meetings, Collaborative leaders spoke in strong opposition to the authority's plan which they criticized for its failure to address residents' concerns and its exorbitant price tag.

While these meetings were proceeding, Collaborative leaders met with a wide range of citizen groups and influential members of the county legislature who controlled half of the votes on the Community Redevelopment Agency (CRA) in hopes of influencing their decision. Over time, a growing number of these organizations appeared before the CRA challenging the housing authority's plan. Among these were the Downtown Memphis Commission, Downtown Neighborhood Association, South Main Neighborhood Association, and the Western Tennessee Tea Party.

In the face of growing citizen and legislative opposition, the housing authority TIF application was placed on "indefinite hold". Frustrated in their effort to secure TIF funding, the housing authority is now seeking to finance the local portion of their plan using a variety of city and county funds. However, in a year when local revenues have fallen short of projections, the housing authority may have trouble doing so.

Hoping to elicit Mayor A.C. Wharton's support for this resident-generated plan, Collaborative members attempted to schedule a meeting with him. When they were unable to do so, even with the assistance of their city councilmembers, for more than two months, the Collaborative forwarded a five-page letter of concerns regarding the breakdown in the local Choice Neighborhood planning process to several high-ranking HUD officials. Following conversations with several HUD officials from Washington, the mayor's office contacted the Collaborative to schedule a meeting to learn more about the Collaborative's alternative plan.

Thirty Collaborative members attended this meeting where four resident leaders were prepared to present their plan's origins, goals and objectives, major programmatic elements, advantages over the city's Heritage Trail Plan, and costs. While waiting nearly ninety minutes for Mayor A.C. Wharton to join them, representatives of the Collaborative used this time to brief the city's Chief Administrative Officer, Police Director, and Neighborhood Services Director regarding the plan's unique features and benefits. When the mayor finally arrived, Collaborative leaders presented their plan and asked for the mayor's support. Stating that he had not yet read the plan, the mayor asked for additional time to carefully review both the housing authority's and the Collaborative's plans prior to the April deadline for submitting city's Choice Neighborhood Implementation Grant applications to the U.S. Department of Housing and Urban Development.

Placing their organizing campaign on hold for several weeks while the Mayor studied their plan, the Collaborative prepared the next phase of their organizing campaign. They formulated a local Ethics Complaint against the housing authority for employing contractors to work on both the planning and development phases of the Choice Neighborhood Project, which is considered a significant conflict of interest in most cities. They also prepared a revised application to the Tennessee Historical Commission requesting the listing of Foote Homes on the National Registry of Historic Places. This request was based upon the pivotal role many former Foote Homes residents (including Dr. Hooks, Rufus Thomas, and Mavis Staples) played in creating the organizational base for the Memphis Freedom Struggle.

While pursuing these efforts, the Collaborative also contacted several national journalists to encourage them to cover this ongoing civil rights struggle. In the event the city chose to ignore the hopes and aspirations of the Vance Avenue community, the Collaborative prepared a Fair Housing Complaint against the Memphis Housing Authority and the U.S. Department of Housing and Urban Development and requested an investigation of the Housing Authority's subversion of the Vance Avenue Choice Neighborhood planning process by the HUD Oversight Committee, chaired by Tennessee's U.S. Senator Bob Corker.

When the Collaborative was informed that the City had quietly submitted the Housing Authority's Heritage Trail Plan to HUD's Choice Neighborhood Implementation Grant Program in September

2013 without informing them— as Mayor Wharton had promised—
they organized an informational picketing and informal meeting
with an Assistant Secretary of HUD who was in Memphis to address
a fair housing conference at the University of Memphis Law School.
They also provided the Secretary of HUD's Office with the results of
their public housing survey that showed strong resident and community support for a preservation-oriented approach to improving
conditions within Foote Homes.

In March 2014, HUD announced its new round of Choice Neighborhood Implementation Grants that did not include funding for
Memphis' Heritage Trail Plan. Local officials were both surprised
and disappointed by HUD's rejection of their proposal given their
record of success securing similar competitive housing grants. The
Collaborative responded to the news by seeking to enter into negotiations with the housing authority to maintain a section of the Foote
Homes complex to accommodate those who wished to stay. The
housing authority's rejection of the Collaborative's efforts to mediate
the conflict, reductions in their Foote Homes maintenance program,
and regular notices to residents urging them to prepare for relocation
took their toll on the Vance community's ongoing organizing efforts.

In February 2015, the Memphis Housing Authority resubmitted
a modified version of their Heritage Trail Plan that was included in
HUD's September 2015 list of Choice Neighborhood Implementation Grantees. By the spring of 2016, the housing authority, with the
help of Section 8 vouchers, was fully engaged in relocating residents
from its last remaining family housing complex. In 2017, the housing
authority began demolition of Foote Homes which was proceeding
unimpeded until the discovery of contaminated soils interrupted
the completion of this process and delayed the construction of the
Heritage Trail Plan's new mixed-income housing.

While organizers of the Collaborative lament the loss of more
than 400 well-designed, constructed, and maintained public housing
units in the heart of the city's downtown, they believe the nearly
ten-year campaign to preserve this historic project produced a
number of positive outcomes. First, it allowed Foote Homes residents
to remain in their homes and in the community that they valued for
a significant period of time. Second, it highlighted the housing

authority's historic relocation problems that put pressure on the agency to improve its case management practices. Third, it saved the city and county (both of which face serious budgetary challenges) from committing $102 million in future real estate tax revenues to a redevelopment project whose primary beneficiaries are private developers and investors. Fourth, it focused the formidable organizing capacity of several faith-based organizations on the educational, employment, housing, and health-care needs of the city's poorest residents. Finally, it created a new expectation among a broad cross-section of Memphis residents and civic leaders that large-scale redevelopment plans, such as the Heritage Trail Plan, which had previously moved forward with little or no public debate, should not be allowed to do so!

ACKNOWLEDGEMENTS

A version of the following essays was published earlier by *Social Policy* in the following issues:

- Equitable Development Comes to DC by Dominic T. Moulden and Gregory D. Squires, *Social Policy*, Fall 2012 v.42#3

- Seeking a Choice for Public Housing Tenants in Memphis, Tennessee by Kenneth M. Reardon, *Social Policy*, Spring 2013 v.43 #1

- One of ACORN's First Battles: Fighting the Freeway in Little Rock, Arkansas by Darcy Pumphrey, *Social Policy*, Fall 2014 v.44 # 3

- Using Community Organizing Strategies to Fight Hospital Debt in Washington by LeeAnn Hall, *Social Policy*, Spring 2015 v.45#2.

- Black Rents and Blank Spots by David Tozzo, *Social Policy*, Fall 2015 v.45 #3.

- Local Communities from Five Countries Allied Against Land-Grabbing by a Transnational Corporation by Eloise Maulet, *Social Policy*, Winter 2016 v.46#4

- Doing the Unthinkable in Cleveland, Ohio by Randy Cunningham, *Social Policy*, Fall 2017 v.47#3.

- Blocking the Council Tax in Bristol by Nick Ballard and Anny Cullum, *Social Policy*, Winter 2017 v.47#4

A version of the following essays and excerpts was published earlier in Community Organizing Handbook #2 from the Institute of Social Justice (copyright 1977) and the 3rd edition, reprinted in 1983. Editors: Meg Campbell, Lina Newhouser, and Wade Rathke.

- ACORN: An Overview of its History, Structure, Methodology, Campaigns, and Philosophy by Steven Kest and Wade Rathke, pages 1 through 9.

    CNA/ACORN, pages 5-6

    Furniture for Families, page 6

Property Taxes '73-'75, pages 6-7

White Bluff Power Plant, pages 7-8

The Ambulance Pledge Card System by Zach Polett, pages 17-18

"Don't Be a Blockhead" is an excerpt drawn from *The People Shall Rule* edited by Robert Fisher, Vanderbilt University Press, 2009.

Chapter Nine, "Don't Be a Blockhead: ACORN, Protest Tactics, and Organizational Scale," by Robert Fisher, Fred Brooks, and Daniel Russell. (page 206)

Part of "Minimum Standards Campaigns" drawn from *Nuts & Bolts: The ACORN Fundamentals of Organizing* by Wade Rathke, Social Policy Press, 2018. (page 349)

AUTHOR AND EDITOR NOTES

John Anderson is the Field and Training Director for ACORN Canada based in Toronto.

Drew Astolfi is a long-time faith and community based organizer. He was the Director of Faith Action for Community Equity from 2005 to 2015. He currently works for the Center for Community Change.

Nick Ballard is a founding staffer and National Coordinator of ACORN United Kingdom based in Bristol, England.

Nik Belanger is the Organizing Director of Virginia Organizing and worked to build the Danville and Martinsville/Henry County chapters.

Fred Brooks teaches social work at Georgia State University. His research centers on policies and interventions designed to decrease inequality and poverty with a particular focus on community and labor organizing. Fred worked for ACORN from 1979 to 1990 managing canvass programs.

Marva Burnett is a day care worker in Toronto, Canada, originally from St. Vincent in the St. Vincent and Grenadines. She is the President of ACORN Canada and currently the President of ACORN International.

Beth Butler is a Director of community organizing at A Community Voice, New Orleans, LA, an affiliate of ACORN International and pillar of the citywide coalition Justice and Beyond. Butler developed ACORN's largest community organization in the South, with a 45-year focus in organizing low-to moderate-income people and organized the rape campaigns in the essay in this book.

Diné Butler worked for ten years as a union organizer with Local 100 United Labor Unions and as an ACORN community organizer in New Orleans and Buenos Aires. Most recently, Diné is in CUNY Hunter's Urban Policy master's program and working with the Fifth Avenue Committee as a Morgan Stanley/ANHD fellow. She is also the Program Director of ACORN's Home Savers Campaign, which uniquely tackles the US affordable housing challenge through corporate campaigns, public-private partnerships, and financial empowerment programs.

Anny Crumble is a founding member of ACORN Bristol, the first Branch of ACORN UK and has been a key leader and organizer ever since. During a four-month internship she headed up the ground operation of the Council Tax campaign referred to in this article.

Randy Cunningham is a steering committee member of the Cuyahoga County Progressive Caucus, long-time tenant organizer, and the author of *Democratizing Cleveland: The Rise and Fall of Community Organizing in Cleveland, Ohio 1975-1985*, 2007.

Judy Duncan founded ACORN Canada in August 2004 and has been its head organizer ever since. Duncan previously worked as lead organizer for Washington ACORN in Seattle. The organization has now grown to over 113,000 members, with seven offices across the country. Judy has an MA in Community and Regional Development from the University of British Columbia.

Robert Fisher teaches community organizing in a graduate level social work program at UCONN. He has been promoting and critiquing organizing since the mid-1970s. *Let The People Decide: Neighborhood Organizing in America* recently appeared in a Chinese edition.

Claire Gallagher is ACORN Canada's Research and Communications Coordinator. Claire has a Community Learning and Development Masters from the University of Glasgow in Scotland.

Steven Kest currently serves as Senior Advisor to the Center for Popular Democracy and before that with SEIU. Previously, Steven worked for ACORN for over thirty-five years in a wide variety of roles, including as Head Organizer of Arkansas ACORN and as Executive Director.

Eloise Maulet works with the transnational campaigning organization ReAct based in Grenoble, France, coordinates the work of the Bollore campaign, and directs the work in Africa for ACORN and its affiliates.

Mike Miller directs ORGANIZE Training Center (OTC) at www.organizetrainingcenter.org. He is the author of *A Community Organizer's Tale: People and Power in San Francisco*, 2009.

Dominic Moulden is a Resource Organizer with ONE DC.

Bill Pastreich was trained by Fred Ross. He was a Peace Corps Volunteer-Chile, Organizer for the United Farm Workers, Director of MWRO, head organizer of NWRO, Director of Cape Cod Health Care Coalition, Director of Cape Cod & Is. Tenants Council, Director of SEIU 767, head organizer for SFOrganize, and head organizer for Building Trades Organizing Program.

Zach Polett wrote this piece while head organizer of Arkansas ACORN based on his experience as regional organizer in Fort Smith. After more than thirty years with ACORN, largely as political director, he is now campaign director for the Public Interest Network, although still based in Little Rock.

Darcy Pumphrey is now the Digital Project Coordinator at the Merrill-Cazier Library of Utah State University in Logan, Utah. She wrote her thesis at the University of North Texas on the Wilbur Mills Expressway development and campaign.

Antonio Raciti is an Assistant Professor of Environmental Planning and Ecological Design at the University of Massachusetts Boston. He was a member of the University of Memphis faculty during the Vance Avenue Collaborative. He is originally from Sicily.

Ken Reardon is a Professor and Director of Urban Planning and Community Development at the University of Massachusetts Boston. He was a member of the University of Memphis faculty who partnered with the Vance Avenue Collaborative in the production of the Vance Avenue Community Transformation Plan. Prior to that he was the head of the Department of Regional and Local Planning at Cornell University in Ithaca, New York.

Rev. Ruth Rinehart is a Unitarian Universalist minister, a former ACORN organizer, advisor to current organizers, and works in every way she can to smash the hetero-normative, ableist, white supremacist, capitalist patriarchy, and is currently based in Colorado.

Daniel Russell is a Professor Emeritus in Political Science at Springfield College. He started researching ACORN and social movement organizations in 1976 doing fieldwork as an ACORN volunteer organizer in New Orleans. His Ph.D. dissertation was published as "Political Organizing in Grassroots Politics."

Joe Szakos has been a community organizer for more than four decades. He served as Executive Director of Virginia Organizing from 1994-2017. He is co-author, with his wife, Kristin Layng Szakos, of *We Make Change: Community Organizers Talk About What They Do—and Why*, Vanderbilt University Press, 2007.

Gregory D. Squires is Professor of Sociology and Public Policy and Public Administration at George Washington University

Author and Editor

Wade Rathke first began organizing almost fifty years ago when he dropped out of college to organize against the Vietnam War. Later he organized welfare recipients in Massachusetts, first in Springfield and then statewide from Boston, before leaving for Arkansas to found ACORN in Little Rock in mid-June 1970. Wade left ACORN after thirty-eight years as its chief organizer in mid-2008, when the organization had more than 100 offices and close to 500,000 members. Now he continues as Chief Organizer of ACORN International, working in Canada, Mexico, Peru, Honduras, India, Kenya, Italy, Cameroon, Scotland, France, and England and with partnerships in Indonesia, Korea, and the Philippines. ACORN International is also organizing unions of hawkers and wastepickers in Delhi, Mumbai, and Benglauru while supporting worker organizations in other countries as well.

Wade is also publisher and editor-in-chief of *Social Policy*, the quarterly journal that has been able to offer a forum for the many voices from organizing, academia, and elsewhere on issues that matter around social change here and abroad.

Wade's first book was *Citizen Wealth: Winning the Campaign to Save Working Families* (2009) published by Berrett-Koehler. In addition, he wrote *The Battle for the Ninth Ward: ACORN, Rebuilding New Orleans, and the Lessons of Disaster* (2011) along with *Global Grassroots: Perspectives on International Organizing* (2011) where he served as editor. Most recently he finished *Nuts & Bolts: The ACORN Fundamentals of Organizing* (2018). Wade writes a daily blog www.chieforganizer.org, also available as a podcast and distributed to radio stations, especially KABF at www.kabf.org in Little Rock, WDSV at wdsv919.org in Greenville (MS), and WAMF at www.wamf.org in New Orleans as well as ACORN's internet station at www.acornradio.org.

He can be reached at chieforganizer@acorninternational.org.

SOCIAL POLICY PUBLICATIONS

Social Policy
The journal *Social Policy* is now completing its 48th year and is published quarterly and on-line at www.socialpolicy.org.

Subscriptions are:
Individuals Print and Online - 2019
Domestic US $65–1 year $110–2 years
Canada/Mexico $75–1 year $130–2 years
Other Countries $80–1 year $145–2 years

Institutions 2019
Domestic USA $285–1 year
Canada/Mexico $315–1 year
Other Countries $340–1 year

Social Policy Press Titles
Lessons from the Field: Organizing in Rural Communities, Joe Szakos and Kristin Layng Szakos (editors). Available $15.00 plus shipping.

The Battle for the Ninth Ward: ACORN, Rebuilding New Orleans, and the Lessons of Disaster, Wade Rathke. Available $20.00 plus shipping or as an e-book.

Global Grassroots: Perspectives on International Organizing, Wade Rathke (editor). Available $20.00 plus shipping or as an e-book.

Guns and Kids: Can We Survive the Carnage, Franklin Strier. Available as an e-book.

Building Power, Changing Lives: The Story of Virginia Organizing, Ruth Berta and Amanda Leonard Pohl. Available $15.00 plus shipping.

Nuts and Bolts: The ACORN Fundamentals of Organizing, Wade Rathke. Available $35.00 or as an e-book.

NOTES

NOTES